# HALCYON

GABRIELE D'ANNUNZIO was born in 1863 in Pescara, on the Adriatic coast of Italy, the son of a wealthy landowner. His first volume of poetry was published in 1879, when he was sixteen. After graduating from the University of Rome, d'Annunzio married and began to write short stories to support his wife and family. His first novel was published in 1889. The marriage ended in 1891, by which time he had moved to Naples. In 1894 d'Annunzio began a love affair with the actress Eleonora Duse, and wrote several plays for her. He was elected to parliament in 1897, but lost his seat in the elections of the following year. Increasingly in debt, d'Annunzio left Italy for France in 1910, but returned at the outbreak of the first world war. He urged the entry of Italy into the war and himself joined the air force, losing an eye in a flying accident. In 1919 d'Annunzio led a small force to seize the town of Fiume, ruling it as a dictator until 1921. D'Annunzio spent the later part of his life at his home on Lake Garda. In 1937 he was made President of the Italian Royal Academy. He died in 1938 and was given a state funeral by Mussolini.

J.G. NICHOLS was born in Liverpool (UK) in 1930. He is a poet, literary critic and translator (particularly from the Italian). His translation of Guido Gozzano's *Colloquies* won the John Florio prize in 1988, and his translation of Petrarch's *Canzoniere* won the Monselice prize in 2000. J.G. Nichols' translation of Giacomo Leopardi's *Canti* is also published in the Fyfield series.

Fyfield*Books* aim to make available some of the great classics of British and European literature in clear, affordable formats, and to restore often neglected writers to their place in literary tradition.

Fyfield*Books* take their name from the Fyfield elm in Matthew Arnold's 'Scholar Gypsy' and 'Thyrsis'. The tree stood not far from the village where the series was originally devised in 1971.

> *Roam on! The light we sought is shining still.*
> *Dost thou ask proof? Our tree yet crowns the hill,*
> *Our Scholar travels yet the loved hill-side*

from 'Thyrsis'

GABRIELE D'ANNUNZIO

# *Halcyon*

Translated with an introduction by
J.G. NICHOLS

Fyfield*Books*

CARCANET

# ACKNOWLEDGEMENTS

In translating *Alcyone* I have used the edition by Frederico Roncoroni (Arnoldo Mondadori, Milan, 1982), with some reference to the text edited by Egidio Bianchetti (in *Versi d'amore e di gloria*, volume 2, Arnoldo Mondadori, Milan, 11th edition, 1980) and to the comments in the selection edited by J.R. Woodhouse (Manchester University Press, 1978).

I am grateful to Michael Schmidt for his advice and criticism.

First published in Great Britain in 1988 by
Carcanet Press Limited
Alliance House
Cross Street
Manchester M2 7AQ

This impression 2003

Introduction, translation and glossary © J.G. Nichols 1988, 2003

A CIP catalogue record for this book is available from the British Library
ISBN 1 85754 693 8

The publisher acknowledges financial assistance from
the Arts Council of England

Printed and bound in England by SRP Ltd, Exeter

# Contents

# Introduction

*The world does not belong to the vainglorious conqueror but to the solitary craftsman. the world, perishable and perennial, was only created so that artistry might transform it into sovereign everlasting shapes. (A hundred and a hundred and a hundred and a hundred pages of the secret book of Gabriele d'Annunzio tempted to die)*

If d'Annunzio is still a name to conjure with, then that is, in this country at least, more on account of his life than of his art. This is a pity, because much of his work is still such as to command respect while his life, though sensational, was often reprehensible, often risible, and sometimes both at the same time. His endless love affairs get tedious, his duelling looks silly, and his military exploits during and after the First World War seem in retrospect to be merely a sort of elegant hooliganism. To do him justice he was never under the spell of Mussolini; but this was because Mussolini and his Fascists came first under the spell of d'Annunzio, or rather of the climate of opinion which d'Annunzio had done so much to form: his seizure of Fiume in 1919 was copied only a few years later, with much more dire results for Italy and Europe, in Mussolini's march on Rome. D'Annunzio the aesthete, the decadent, is a more intelligent and intelligible person altogether than d'Annunzio the man of action, but any assessment of his life has to take account of the fact that he was, as Mario Praz has so shrewdly observed, a barbarian and a decadent at the same time. The combination is frequently disconcerting.

Fortunately, enjoyment of *Halcyon*, by general consent the best of d'Annunzio's volumes of poems, does not depend upon a knowledge of, still less any admiration for, his life. When *Halcyon* was first published, at the end of 1903, its author was already forty and famous: *Il piacere*, which ranks with *A rebours* and *The Picture of Dorian Gray* as a novel of the Decadence, had appeared in 1889, and d'Annunzio had published other novels, short stories, plays, and many volumes of poetry since his first great success at the age of sixteen. He had already been in politics (the first poem in *Halcyon* expresses his disgust with it), although his deepest political involvement and his military career were still to come. *Halcyon* is the expression of a respite from his public life,

7

a holiday book, written, as its author tells us, in a happy region where 'there was no other cross except that of the poles suspended over the flood in a miracle of gold'. These are the poles from which fishing-nets were hung:

> The mouth – a lake
> of salt and coloured like
> sea seen through stilted huts,
> and through enormous nets
> hanging from poles and struts
> arranged like crosses – is quite still.
>
> 'Noon'

They had already been described in 'Mouth of the Arno': 'Great calyxes are growing from the water / in open-work of finest golden thread.' When reading *Halcyon* we do best to trust such images; in the words of a poet who, as it happens, visited Schloss Duino not very long before d'Annunzio bombed it, 'Wisse das Bild' (Know the image). The author of *Halcyon* need not disturb us too much, for the subject of his book is not d'Annunzio but 'naked Summer blazing in the sky'.

An acquaintance with d'Annunzio's life and his work might lead us to expect certain qualities which are fortunately hardly to be found in *Halcyon*. It is a pity that the book begins on a somewhat strident note with 'The truce', a poem which only towards its end modulates into the manner most characteristic of the book. Generally there is here comparatively little trace of that d'Annunzio whom Dino Campana mocked as 'the bardic gramophone', lecturing, hectoring and threatening. It is true that political considerations are not entirely absent. There are a few occasions when the reader with some knowledge of Italian Fascism will have a sudden unexpected frisson which other readers could well miss. The malarial lands which d'Annunzio in 'First dithyramb' foresees being harvested are in fact the Pontine marshes, which long after the date of this poem were drained and farmed under Mussolini. Then the term used for the Mediterranean in 'Orphic anniversary', 'Mare Nostrum' ('Our Sea', and in Italian not Latin in the original), not only looks back to an ancient Roman reality but also looks forward, whether consciously or not, to one of Mussolini's vain hopes. Nevertheless, the occasional intrusion of the outside world with its political problems and barbarous means for settling them serves mainly to throw the idyllic nature of the poetry into stronger relief:

> ...all Versilia takes a golden hue
> with which the heart is torn. You never were,
> Pania, as beautiful as you are now
> in this last hour!
>
> O Tyrrhene Sea, O Lower Sea, the Lighthouse
> kindles its sleepless eye upon your mirror;
> and you are guarded also by tremendous
> steel ships, watched over
>
> out of La Spezia, just behind Cape Crow
> which is defensive for all Italy...
>
> 'Envoi'

It is interesting, although less and less surprising as we come to realise the subtlety of which d'Annunzio is capable in *Halcyon*, to notice that the poem in which he is possibly most politically persuasive, 'The loggia', could easily be read and enjoyed with little awareness of its political content. Part of what d'Annunzio is expressing in this poem is the Irredentist feeling which led to Italy's entry into the First World War, but the tone of the poem is gentle and nostalgic:

> September, how your little brother April
> cast flowers upon the ruins of San Marco
> at Capodistria...
>
> The nests are now deserted in the loggia,
> and of the bunches of sorb-apples only
> the canes remain perhaps while slip-knots hold.
> And such the way of speaking in the shadow
> Rialto, Cannaregio come to mind.
>
> A dove is moaning on the frieze outside.

That d'Annunzio is deliberately avoiding overt political engagement in *Halcyon* is clear from 'The youngster', one of d'Annunzio's most extended expressions of his poetic ideals while writing this book, where the situation is summarized neatly: 'A brazen trumpet blares from far away.'

Qualities which one might expect to find in a decadent writer are much more obvious. There is a pervasive feeling of living on the ruins of past civilisations and past certainties:

> A temple comes in sight, a ruined mound
> ruptured by crazy roots
> that wander off. The ancient gods are finished.
> Their mutilated statues lie around,
> fallen from pediments
> and darkly robed in ivy-berry-clusters.
>
> 'The youngster'

There is a sense too in which d'Annunzio as a poet is living off such ruins, for much of the material of his poetry is drawn from the past. Attempts to recall the past can sometimes result in a poem that is charming in a rather faded way, as I think happens with 'Beatitude' which is much more reminiscent of Rossetti than of Dante. More often we feel that d'Annunzio, as he creates his own myths or modifies old ones to suit his purposes, is engaged in the common post-Nietzschean attempt of the modern poet to create his own values. Sometimes he is strikingly successful in recreating the ancient pagan world and its values, though 'values' is too abstract a word for the places and people he presents to us. 'The coronal of Glauco' is particularly successful in this respect:

> A guest who's not ungrateful, I am Gorgo,
> bringing with me the scented Cyclades,
> and bringing grapes and spices too in these
> fine light and airy linens from Amorgo.

But this takes us beyond any idea of decadence, of that sort of decadence which keeps, not so much popping up, as languidly raising its head throughout the book:

> I pick out a sarcophagus, one sculptured
> on three sides with a battling Alexander;
> earth it contains now, and an oleander.
>
> 'Roman sarcophagus'

In a passage strikingly reminiscent of Pater, a passage which shows incidentally the poet's limited power of abstract thought stretched to its utmost, d'Annunzio was later to write: 'This is my certainty. nothing counts but the moment, nothing matters in the order of the Universe but the moment: that moment which deep art expresses, which perhaps the art of the future will express, convinced that all the rest is nothing' *(A hundred and a hundred and a hundred and a hundred pages of the secret book of Gabriele d'Annunzio tempted to die)*. In *Halcyon* these moments are frequently captured in a manner that draws attention to itself as much as to the matter it expresses. This is seen in d'Annunzio's obvious delight in words, particularly proper nouns:

> May mullet redden on our low straw table
> among the carp-like dentex and umbrina,
> wine from Vernazza in its bulging bottle,
> wine from Corniglia.
>
> 'August festival'

There are examples on every page. Particularly noticeable is the almost religious reverence with which he handles, fondles rather, the names of places:

> We heard on the waste Gombo in a dream
> Triton's enormous twisted trumpet blown where
> Luni was echoing the sonic boom
> to Populonia.
>
> 'Orphic anniversary'

The sonnet 'Ocean laurel' is particularly interesting because it consists largely of a catalogue of plants, a catalogue which leaves us at the end dubious as to which d'Annunzio admires the more – the plants or their names. Nevertheless, such a delight in language, and particularly in proper names, is after all only an exaggeration of what is normal for a poet, what d'Annunzio calls in relation to Petrarch 'sensuous love of the word'. What is remarkable in *Halcyon* is the extent to which the whole style tends to draw attention to itself, almost as though *ars est demonstrare artem*. There is such ostentation in this description of the shore near Pisa:

> earth delicate and strong
> as though it were outlined
> by the ever-certain hand
> of the potter whence is born
> that vase which is most precious

11

> although it does not glitter
> or weigh a ton, pure form,
> pride of the dining-table
> and of the Etruscan tomb,
> the flower of every form
> in art's unaltering sky...
>                          'The camels'

D'Annunzio does not quite compare the beauty of the shore with the beauty of his poem; but one expects him to any moment, and indeed we are encouraged to do so if we read this poem after reading 'The oleander' which contains a similar image of weight-lessness when it mentions 'the Ode, made out of everlasting words, / and lighter than a garland of wild olive...'. 'The wave' makes finally explicit what is implicit in many of these poems. 'The wave' enjoys itself imitating the movement of the sea:

> The wave the wind unleashes
> falls apart,
> rushing into the hollow
> of the sounding furrow;
> it foams, it whitens,
> like scented flowers, it brightens,
> it sweeps a floating meadow
> of alga and sea-lettuce;
> it stretches itself,
> it rolls and tumbles, gallops;
> it stumbles
> into a wave the wind
> has shaped of a different kind...

It does this sort of thing for a hundred lines, and then the poem admits it has been speaking of itself: 'So, Muse, I sang the praise / of my Extended Stanza.'

One of the traditional subjects of poetry is of course poetry itself – Horace and Yeats immediately spring to mind – but there is more to it than that in *Halcyon*. We sense in this book, as we do I think in much of the later Rilke, that the poems talk of themselves because in a world where values are so uncertain the only reality left is art, especially the supreme expressive art of poetry. One difference is that in Rilke the poetry often has an overt meta-

12

physical content and he spells out his belief that the world must be created by poetry, whereas d'Annunzio generally leaves that to be understood. The man who said that a book of criticism should above all be an excellent book of prose, 'a work of art added to a work of art' (so damning in advance large tracts of twentieth-century writing) had little time for theory, and he was more interested in the world of the senses than in generalizing about what might lie behind it. In Pater's words:

> Every moment some form grows perfect in hand or face; some tone on the hills or the sea is choicer than the rest; some mood of passion or insight or intellectual excitement is irresistibly real and attractive to us, – for that moment only. Not the fruit of experience, but experience itself, is the end.    (The Renaissance)

In *Halcyon* we have what has been described as a 'solar diary' of a summer spent in that part of Tuscany which lies between Florence and the Tyrrhenian Sea. The poems recall specific times and places; but, more importantly, they evoke the feelings, the memories, the myths these places bring to mind. This is not a diary written to record the actions and opinions of its author (although these must surface from time to time): rather the author, so often elsewhere egotistic and bombastic, becomes here just a voice to record impressions. The range and subtlety of that voice are worth looking at in some detail.

*Halcyon* is a long book, composed of many kinds of poem in many verse-forms, from dithyrambs to elegies, and from sonnets to free verse. Nevertheless, it is all highly organized, in ways that are worth at least indicating, although a full account of the organization would make a book in itself. Most obviously, the poems are arranged in a general chronological order, not of composition of course, but of subject and mood, starting with the early summer, moving on to summer at its height, and finishing in the early autumn. This method has the incidental effect of placing some of d'Annunzio's best poems, his melancholy laments for the fading of summer like 'Dreams of distant places', near the end of the volume. I do not wish to imply that it is necessary to read the poems in the order in which they occur – or even perhaps to read all the poems, for their quality does vary considerably – because this chronological order applies rather to blocks of poems than to individual pieces, and it is anyway only the most crude form of organization used. It helps to be aware of it.

Much more subtle are the correspondences between poems in the same group: the reader can have a happy time noticing the various links between the nine sonnets of 'The coronal of Glauco', or seeing how the 'Summer madrigals' form a whole made up of an introduction and then two smaller groups of five poems each, each of those smaller groups with internal links between the poems of which it is made up and external links with the other group. Then the reader might like to see what the 'Second dithyramb' has to say about Glauco, or – intrigued by the swallow at the end of 'Summer madrigals' – notice all the other references to swallows in the book. A glance at the glossary will give a rough idea of how d'Annunzio tends to recur to the same themes and images and people. Often it is true that the best commentary on one of these poems is another one of them. For this reason it is perhaps best, after all, to read all the poems, even the inferior ones. Some information may be given (which is one of the advantages of reading 'Second dithyramb' in connection with 'The coronal of Glauco'), or one poem may serve to introduce another (as 'A goddess of the shore' introduces 'Undulna'), or the connection between the poems may be, and very often is, much more subtle. Suppose we place two quotations together:

> ... the colourless and silent mouth
> of the little stream that springs in Falterona.
> > 'Mouth of the Arno'

> The millwheel sounds like thunder.
> One spring is solitary in Falterona.
> > 'The tributaries'

Each of these passages has a mysterious effect which, although impossible to explain, has something to do, I think, with a contrast in the first between the calmness of the Arno at its mouth and the energetic start that river makes, a contrast in the second between the millwheel with its connotations of human labour and the remoteness from such things of the Arno at its source, and a sense in both passages that great things can have obscure and humble origins. Each passage has its own individual effect, but each reads better if we know the other as well. Both gain also, of course, if the reader is familiar, as any Italian reader would be, with the mention of the Arno in the fourteenth canto of the *Purgatorio*: '...through central Tuscany there wanders / a little stream that springs in Falterona...'.

The range of mood in *Halcyon* is very great. These poems can be lyrically enthusiastic, and maintain this lyricism over many lines, as in 'August festival' (p.157); they can be idyllic (e.g. 'Between two Arnos', p.66); they can be nostalgic and elegiac (e.g. 'Dreams of distant places', p.207). They can also, not so happily, be portentous, particularly in 'First dithyramb' and 'Fourth dithyramb'. On the whole the dithyrambs, while they serve a useful purpose in marking off different sections of the work, add jarring notes rather than acceptable variety to *Halcyon*: they shout too loudly. A sense of awe, an almost Greek sense of the numinous, which is I think part of what d'Annunzio has in mind in the dithyrambs, is much better conveyed in the quiet tones of 'The flautist', one of the sonnets of 'The coronal of Glauco':

> ...all oblivious of the dreadful doom,
> I dare within my garden now and then
> even beneath the laurel blow this flute.
>
> I often turn and look about me for
> the god who might be quickly manifest.
> And yet this lip is never known to tremble.

As a sharp contrast, it is worth noticing that d'Annunzio is able, when he wishes, to be playful, as in 'Versilia':

> Don't be afraid, man with the blue-
> green eyes! I'm just Versilia bursting
> free from her wood-nymph's bark, and thirsting.
> Ready to let you touch me too!

This playfulness is most welcome because it is not a quality always associated with d'Annunzio, whose lack of a strong sense of humour can even lead him, although not very often, to fall into absurdity. He is fond of using for the sea the metonymy 'sale' (salt); when he calls it 'sale amaro' (bitter salt) then he is unintentionally, and quite inappropriately, calling it Epsom salts. It must be admitted that humour is not his forte, while irony (so beloved

15

of modern poets and their critics) hardly gets a word in edgeways; but a light touch, not only a delicacy with words but also some subtlety in the poet's attitude to his themes, is not uncommon in *Halcyon*, as 'The coronal of Glauco' shows throughout.

D'Annunzio's range in his more localized effects is also impressive. Again and again sensuous impressions are masterfully conveyed, as in 'Stabat nvda Aestas' (p.136) or, to take a particularly ostentatious example, 'Ocean laurel' (p.163). D'Annunzio can also be evocative in a much more delicate, and at the same time more far-reaching way. The swallows in 'By the side of the Affrico on an evening in June after rain' appear first in an impressionistic representation of their flight:

> O swallows, black and white, between the night
> and dawn, evening and night, O white and black
> nocturnal guests along the Affrico!
> Their breasts touch very lightly in low flight
> on soft wet grass...

Then we have an image which is not only sensuous but also abstract as it conveys the poet's pleasure and pride in the practice of his art: 'Is not the flight around about my temples / weaving fresh garlands?' Then there is an image which records a sensuous illusion in order to convey an abstract reality:

> They linger as their nests were out of mind,
> and on the margin when they have flitted past
> the rustle of their wings appears to stay.

Finally the swallows and the poet are brought together as artificers about to start work, the swallows on their nests and the poet on his book: 'The whole earth looks like clay / ready and offered for the work of love...'.

It is an important feature of *Halcyon* that, while its best and most characteristic poems are free from didacticism, they do not content themselves with conveying sense-impressions, admirably though they do this. The poet is inspired not only by the landscape of Tuscany, though that is his most immediate and obvious love in this book; what his senses apprehend is fused with the memories left by earlier sense-impressions and with his strong feeling for history; he reaches back, behind the Tuscan landscape which is in front of his eyes, to the glorious Latin past

16

and to memories of his travels in Greece and the memorials of a
glorious past which are to be found there. In 'Orphic anniversary'
we have a shore in Tuscany, a figure from ancient Greek mythol-
ogy, and two old Etruscan towns to set the scene for a poem
dedicated to an English poet who had been drowned nearby
some eighty years earlier:

> We heard on the waste Gombo in a dream
> Triton's enormous twisted trumpet blown where
> Luni was echoing the sonic boom
> to Populonia.

Those Etruscan names are repeated in 'To Gorgo' where there is
a similar mélange of landscapes and languages and cultures:

> Dance me that supple dance out of Ionia
> now while the Apuan Alps are turning red
> and the Tyrrhenian sighs and colours up.

> Hellas is here – Luni to Populonia!
> It is as though I watched you while you poured
> me wine of Greece in an Etruscan cup.

So while it is true to say that these are poems set in one compara-
tively small part of Tuscany, and while that area provides a focus
for them, it is also true that the poet's mind ranges far beyond
this area in space and in time: the poems are not local in any
restricting sense. The continual movement between the outer
world of Tuscany and the inner world of memories makes these
poems far more than mere sense-impressions: values are con-
veyed, most often – although by no means always – aesthetic
and artistic ones.

A glance at d'Annunzio's figures of comparison leads us to a
similar conclusion. At their worst these figures are so far-fetched
as to be obscure: 'As Summer lives with gold inside her mouth,
/ the Arno carries silence to its mouth' ('The tenzon'). This sort
of thing is rare however. What is much more common is figures
which are certainly conceited, too conceited for some tastes, but
perfectly lucid, as in these lines referring to Michelangelo:

> The Alps were rising, all their thousand summits,
> with the momentum of as many eagles,

such bursting forth of such impetuous strength
from out their stubborn viscera of marble
whence he who did not wish for human offspring
extracted his imperishable children.

'The oleander'

A certain preciosity in the images is not uncommon:

He speaks, and between two bits
of wood weaves shining straw,
as though he were a bard stretching his strings,
created from the guts of little lambs,
between the arms of his lyre.

'The bard without a lyre'

Occasionally we may feel rather uncertain but inclined, perhaps through sheer laziness, to take d'Annunzio's word for it:

. . . that stone which is said to be 'serene'
(much of it comes from Monte Cèceri)
a flawless stone, whose colour somewhat tends
to blue, almost the shade rainwater has
in which a leaf of dyer's woad is boiled.

'Works and days'

Anyone who has seen it will vouch for the blueness of the famous 'pietra serena', but how many could vouch for the accuracy of the comparison? In contrast there are comparisons which are surprising but so clearly accurate that they give unalloyed pleasure:

So I reclined my cheek and, warm as blood,
out of the twisted hollow of my ear
came the sea-water gushing all at once.

'The oleander'

It must be said also that this pleasing accuracy is not limited to simple figures conveying simple sensations. The beginning of 'Fvrit aestvs' triumphantly disproves this: 'A hawk's call clashes with the colour of pearl: / the sky is torn as one might tear a veil.' The pun in 'clashes' is not just a bow to the fashion for synaesthesia: it emphasizes the disturbing nature of the hawk's cry at the same time as, in looking forward to 'the colour of pearl', it emphasizes that image of the serenity which is broken; and the rather biblical image in the second line is not a mere variation on the theme of the first, for the sense of revelation is most appropriate to this poem and indeed to the book as a whole.

Most interesting of all perhaps are the occasions when comparisons are indeed made, but mere collocation is more important:

> The ear of corn, inclined
> to offer itself to man,
> the mountain giving rock out of its womb –
> though this be close at hand,
> that other distant, one
> so slender and the other massive – seem
> to come together in an air of calm,
> like your pursed lips and the melodious reed,
> like loved and lover on a grassy bed,
> like your swift fingers and the seven stops...
>
> 'The youngster'

In this passage, which continues for another eleven lines and is in many ways characteristic of the book, the poet is more concerned with naming than comparing, naming some of his dominant images, and naming them in celebration, for celebration, delight in mere existence, is at the heart of *Halcyon*.

We can see now why the dominant figure of speech in the book is personification, for this is a device which allows a writer to develop an image at length until it takes on a life of its own (indeed to do just that is of the essence of personification) far removed from a mere set of simple correspondences. A personification may be merely sketched in a few words: 'Now coming down Pietrapana / is rapid September with his flute...' ('Versilia'). Or the personification may be developed at greater length:

> Mildest September, the Flute-player
> moving through orchards of our land,
> eyes violet like wistaria,
> youthful of face, curls all around,
>
> scatters his brightness far and wide,
> sounding through two bones of a crane –
> stretched in the shadow of the red
> fruits of the arbutus – his tune.
>
> 'Undulna'

If the personification is developed at sufficient length, and in sufficient detail, then the writer may go so far as to create a myth. This is what happens in the poems from which the above two quotations are taken. To say that Versilia personifies a region in Tuscany and Undulna d'Annunzio's poetic imagination is perfectly true and also utterly inadequate to the complex richness of these poems. D'Annunzio is here, to use Sir Philip Sidney's words, 'making things either better than Nature bringeth forth, or, quite anew, forms such as never were in Nature . . .' *(An apology for poetry)*.

It is of the essence of myth that its significance cannot be adequately explained in other terms; this is of course why we need myths. The same is often true of the detail in *Halcyon*, and even in poems which are not creating myths but concerned on the face of it with description. I mean those passages, and they are not rare, which are compelling because they arouse such a sense of mystery and awe and of inexplicable illumination:

> And in the orchards, silent otherwise,
> of the white monks, defunct, the bees are buzzing;
> the gods that live inside the cells are pagan,
> the Maenads always tear apart their victim,
> Anaximander thinks, and from the wall
> is heard the sequence of the Arval Brethren.
> 'Enos Lases iuvate.' A honey-bee
> goes in where Julia's solid locks beguile.
>
> It shuts itself inside a cell-like curl.
> 'Dreams of distant places'

## The truce

Despot, we went, we fought, and we were ever
faithful to your commandments. You could see
our weapons and our sinews had some vigour.

Despot, benevolent Despot, please concede
that this your warrior rest in shade of laurel,
and feel the grass beneath his naked feet,

and consecrate his very finest sorrel
to raging Rivers and towards the dawn
be happy like the Centaur in the fable.

O Despot, he will then be young again!
Give him the streams the woods the fields the mountains
the heavens, and he will be young again!

Cleansed of all human stench in icy fountains,
but one thing he will ask for in his rest:
that he be ringed around by wide horizons.

The winds and rays will weave a novel dress
in which the flesh may feel itself untrammelled
and bound about released from strain and stress.

You know: obeying you, Unconquerable,
how long we stayed at war, steady bold free,
and never said at heart 'Why take such trouble?'

hopeless of winning; never once did we
show signs of being sad or ill at ease,
because your will upheld us mightily.

Master, you know we did it all to please.
Although the dreadful stench of humankind
oppressed us like a sluggish herd of cows;

most when the mob became a sort of blind
and cumbersome Chimera so foul-smelling
my collar seemed to tighten all around.

Ideals of Life ideals of Death were falling
like lightning flashes on dead flesh in vain,
with all the enigmas of our cryptic calling.

There was no food for bestial hunger in
that fearful beauty; hear the dull beast bellow,
irate, unmoving where rough straw is strewn.

Yet if once for a wonder some sharp quarrel,
made all of gold, struck hard and pierced its hide
right to the heart, the shuddering was dreadful!

And you would say within us: 'The divine
will come to life inside this tiresome monster.
Impress on it the novel mode of life.'

And so we persevered in all our honest
attempts to please you, O our Emperor;
and neither claw nor beak had power upon us.

And then directly from our hidden fire
arose an inextinguishable peal
of laughter, like the brazen trumpet's blare.

And so, each time the filthy animal
insulted us, this laugh rose clear to cleave
the air like crystal ringing from the soul.

A lonely joy! Even the abject slave,
who feeds on crumbs that trickle from the board,
would – from a distance – bark at us and rave;

the crooked pimp, long rotten and decayed
in all his vice, from filthy alleyways
called to us with the sign his finger made.

O Despot, such the comfort that you always
give the great heart, great heart to whom great wrong
is virtue's spur and insult is but praise!

His solitude to him is revelling.
He lends his works to Time, hurt by no scorn,
sensing himself an unexhausted spring.

You warned your pupil: 'Lay your hand upon
not worms in dung but – fitter far for you
to strangle – serpents of Laocoön.'

And so he heeded all the warnings you
gave him, always faithful to each command
of yours, in greatest things, in small things too.

Despot, permit him now to stay his hand,
slacken his bowstring, and enraptured hear those
tunes that are fashioned by the rushing wind!

He has worked and obeyed. He has seen heroes
in asphodel. Now he is taken by
the Fauns – he hears them laughing in the myrtles –

and naked Summer blazing in the sky.

# The youngster

Son of the Olive, son of the Cicada,
what garden of what Faun
was where you picked the reeds from which you wrought
your flute, your double flute with seven stops?

The garden of the country god inside
the old villa on the slope
of Camerata after death abandoned?
Or where the Affrico's long liquid line
furrows the pale landscape
and every field has cypresses about?
Here, where the Mensola runs wildly out,
a bridge across its back?
There, where Ombrone, hot upon the track
of Ambra, has Lorenzo sing his ardour?

At times I can imagine that you picked
reeds for that pipe inside
those walls the Arno parts, in the Rucellai
Gardens, where late barbarity has choked
off short the Florentine
Muse who applauded all the vanished year
the famous laurels, the clear
fountains, the echoes from illustrious caverns,
when over out of Greece eternal Sirens
arrived with Plato in the Flowering City.

No doubt they saw you – Luca della Robbia,
and Donatello too,
while fashioning the white cathedral choirs.
The many-thousand-fruited Cornucopia
under the chisel's blow
was made to weigh the sacred garlands down.
You moved to melodies that were your own,
a naked pagan youth,

24

as lively in the marble as if you
were floating in the air to lead the dancers.

Son of the Olive, son of the Cicada,
now with your sounding pipe
you are enchanting to the light-green lizard
whose living flanks upon the sharp flint shudder,
and throb in sheer delight,
and all in perfect measure with your sound.
Do you not understand,
perhaps, the mind of this most silent creature?
You incline towards it; and it shows no fear;
you modulate your music with its colours.

You modulate with breeze and shade and light,
with water, and with twig,
with ear of corn, with human hand that scythes it,
and with the gentle dove in pure white flight,
with the shy bullock which
arches its back and does it with some grace,
with cloud that moves across
the hill, as though a thought should overwhelm
a peaceful face, with the vine's love for the elm,
the bee's proficiency, the waves of odours.

All voices are apparent in your sound,
just as in them you are
sown broadcast, with the stops that close and open.
Though all things move obedient to your hand
it seems, you also are
happy to answer the eternal motion,
in ignorant recognition
of every single truth the shadow hides.
If you should question earth, the sky replies;
talk with the waters, you are heard by flowers.

O you, innumerable flower of all
this flourishing life, the human
flower of the innocent and godlike art,
we pray to see in you our naked soul,

beseeching it to form in
its wildest flights a shape that looks like you!
All this abundant teeming plenitude
shakes in the lightest notes
your innocent and youthful breath creates,
and man with all his fervour and his fever.


## II


And now your melody
creates the valley, like a happy thought
of peace. Such music from your double flute:
from one frail reed the light, from one the shadow!

The ear of corn, inclined
to offer itself to man,
the mountain giving rock out of its womb –
though this be close at hand,
that other distant, one
so slender and the other massive – seem
to come together in an air of calm,
like your pursed lips and the melodious reed,
like loved and lover on a grassy bed,
like your swift fingers and the seven stops,

like the sea and the mouths of rivers,
like feathers black and white upon one bird,
like oleander flowers and your pale forehead,
like the grape and the vine-leaves,
like the swallow's nest and over it the eaves,
like the fountain and the urn,
like the wet clay and the thumb,
like honey in those combs of yours and wax,
like the fire and stubble when it starts to crackle,
like footpath and footprint,
like the light touching the dark at every point.

## III

Sleep overcame me here beside the fountain.
The swarm was all discordant:
it had two queens; it was hanging like two tawny
breasts. And the bell-like bronze was ringing out.

And in my dream I saw you, mellow flautist.
You had struggled naked, even
against the torrent which was wild for rapine.
You had gathered up a feather from a hawk
which high in the silent heaven
with gyring cries was wounding all the air.
And you had thrown your double reed-pipe far
away, with its seven stops, from your musical fingers.
And you were sitting bent, your brows all wrinkled,
a youngster ready to fight,
busily making bows with which to shoot,
and making them from pliant hazel-wood.

## IV

You had the skill to choose the gleaming queen
from the swarm that was so divided,
and to laugh aloud, magnificent and wild,
extinguishing the sounding sterile drone.

Your hand, stained by crushed leaves of honey-balm,
reached over and unloosed
the unwanted queen, and crushed her well and truly.
Projecting like the nipple on a breast,
one queen was left, one calm
crowned head of craftsmen working in sweet stuff.
Then you went boldly off,
sounding across the trefoiled countryside,
crowned with an ivy-crown and crowned with pride,
within the golden cloud of honey-bees.

# V

The springing water fringed by your black lashes
has turned into a seeing smiling eye;
the billows on your neck are fashioned by
the curling maidenhair.

In secret you are made from what is fresh.
There's latex for your limbs,
smooth latex running through the humid fibres.
Your spirit, like the bitter willow, comes –
but without bitterness –
from founts recalling nymphs of spring and river;
it seems all streaming water
is streaming through invisible roots and stock.
If your blue eyes have lashes that are black,
black stems uphold the bright green maidenhair.

Your twin reeds are transfigured into clear
glass, whence the lazy notes
drip like the drops which leave the hydroscope.
The colubers, their backs covered in spots,
vipers and asps draw near,
all kinds of snakes, cerastes and green hydras.
Silent, uncoiled, unspiralled,
the serpents standing up drink in your charm.
Only their bifid tongues from time to time
are quivering like the quivering maidenhair.

Up to your very knees in the obscure
lymph, you are modulating
your lazy song for your envenomed flock.
It looks as though your hazy feet are making
a twisted root, down where
some grassy substance grows instead of legs.
But, up above, your flesh
blooms on the surface water-lily-like.
If your blue eyes have lashes that are black,
black too are the stalks of the bright green maidenhair.

## VI

Since water can be seen to brim your eyes,
since latex courses all your body through,
no wonder that you live in marbles too,
and make a home inside the Doric column.

Nature and Art, one god who has two faces,
conduct you at your most harmonious pace
through all the fields throughout this spotless Country.
Not marking off one from the other face,
you hear the hidden heartbeat as it pulses
in single strength inside the double figure.
With you, O naked creature,
I'd climb the hallowed rock and on the highland
offer in sacrifice our olive garland
and lay it on that everlasting altar.

Return with me to Hellas – all a sculpture
where hardest stone is offspring of the light
and thought has all the clearness of the air.
Then, as we navigate the moonless night,
we shall observe the seabanks as they glitter
with all the brightness of the day retained.
You will impress the sand
of Phalerum with footprints. And then we,
sole guests, shall hear sing to Antigone
Sophocles' nightingales close by Colonus.

In the Propylaea we shall see the gates
of Day thrown open, in the columned gap
all of the sky of Attica rejoicing;
the Erechtheum – its nocturnal group
in blackening robes, the breathing stone supports,
the maidens standing still like votive urns.
Through all we see there runs
the City's power, running through all the veins
of living marble where Athene reigns,
holding in harmony earth sky and ocean.

29

You won't have had such joy from any tree
as from that column, still untouched by time,
holding the rays of sunlight in its fluting.
There, when the flight of steps is overcome
by that one column's shadow, you will be,
throned on the top step with your Tuscan reeds.
The wingless Victory
may hear you, spoiled of ivory and gold;
winged Victory too, by whom the bull is pulled;
that Victory also who undoes her sandals.

Be silent! Joy has reached its very peak.
Look at Mount Parnes, graceful in the sky!
Look at Hymettus, heavy-dewed with honey
and agile as that youth, it seems to me,
who, dressed in succinct chlamys or short cloak,
bestrides a horse in the Panathenaea.
It was from the Aegean
this mountain of the bees rose into life,
so now its body senses all the time
the undulation of those living waters.

Bay of Aegina! Fostering Salamis
of doves and heroes! The white dusty road
leading through Demeter's ruins to Eleusis!
Oh glory of Pentelicus whose side
is wounded with two quarries! Harmonies
made of the glaucous olive and white rock!
Each gulf is fashioned like
a lyre. Now listen, flautist. On Hymettus
the shadow stretches out. In violet
the mountain murmurs like the scented hive.

VII

I hear him run through gloomy cypresses;
my heart is full of fear.
He calls indeed, but far
off, lonely in the wood, running away.

The sound is changed that comes from his sweet reed;
the heart trembles to hear;
it jumps at shrubs which rustle underfoot:
then, fearful at the roaring of its blood,
it can hear nothing more,
foreboding some deep mourning far away.
'Graceful youngster,' I pray,
'oh do not run so fast
that I can't catch you!' And my voice is lost.
He goes melodiously. He goes away.

Beyond the cypresses some holm-oaks blacken,
old boles pitted and scarred.
High in the sky above white clouds are grazing.
From time to time where the confusions thicken
some insubstantial cloud
is caught by savage branches, birds of prey.
I hear the reed-pipes play
from shade to shade and groan,
hoarse like the calling dove, and always moan,
moving from branch to branch, moving away.

'O youngster, if I could I would arrest
your flight, I am so fond
of you the finest flourish of my spirit!
But turn your head towards me once at least,
if ever I made a garland
for you the offspring of my melancholy!
Now with your melody
there goes something divine
which came to me as 'twere the unforeseen
return of childhood from so far away.

One last time, make me offer you a crown,
though only of black cypress,
and be with you throughout the joyless evening!'
He makes, within the fickle waves of sound,
one of his finest gestures,
who is the very spirit of the spring:
he turns, not answering

but with a smile my prayer.
And should the music pause, I hear my fear,
the while from shade to shade he moves away.

I stumble on a spring the earth receives
in a deep reservoir
of peace – a place a holm-oak shades like night.
'O youngster, stop! You'll imitate the leaves
and waters, and once more,
with all your changing notes, day's silent times.
Let's sit upon the side.
And make me see the image
of you so youthful up against the image
of me in that dark glass!' He moves away.

He has turned his face towards me for the last
time, and he moves away,
light, flighty as Favonius – the same air.
The sun declines, the regions of the west
flare up, and suddenly
all of the wood is one enormous pyre.
The clouds, themselves on fire,
inflame the holm-oaks' branches,
like airy maidens rousing wild desire.
A brazen trumpet blares from far away.

A temple comes in sight, a ruined mound
ruptured by crazy roots
that wander off. The ancient gods are finished.
Their mutilated statues lie around,
fallen from pediments
and darkly robed in ivy-berry-clusters.
The scent of incense gathers
from twisting mastic-tree
and terebinth. 'Son, if you care for me,
stay in this sacred place!' He moves away.

'I'll set the columns up in all their candour,
and with them build once more
the altar where you'll be the only god.

For you I shall adorn it with a splendour
of art not seen before.
To be a wonder-worker is my trade.
You I shall praise inside
temple and breast. Through me
you'll live! You I shall crown immortally!'
In the broad evening blaze he moves away.

He runs into the flames on the horizon.
Brother perhaps of stars?
Or has he been converted to my dream?
'I'll search for you, I'll search upon the highland,
I'll search for you in harsh
rapacious torrents where you will be cleansed.
And I shall find you changed,
your reed-pipes laid apart,
busily making bows with which to shoot,
and making them from pliant hazel-wood.'

## By the side of the Affrico
## on an evening in June after rain

Grace of the sky, how easily you're found
clearly reflected in the watered earth,
as though a soul made beautiful by weeping!
Grace smiling at us from a thousand and
more than a thousand mirrors, come to birth
from cloud, as pleasure comes to birth from weeping,
like music you are creeping
into my song, not fashioned to surcease,
through me transfigured into such deep peace
for one who listens.

Moon, scarcely crescent in the sky, as slight
and slight curving as a girl's eyebrow,
slight as the pith that runs through some young reed,
so that the lightest branch hides you from sight
and if my eye should lose you once I doubt
to find you once again, being dream-blurred,
Luna, that stream which word-
lessly is coming down through grassy banks
sees you and smiles through every blade of grass,
alone to you lonely.

O swallows, black and white, between the night
and dawn, evening and night, O white and black
nocturnal guests along the Affrico!
Their breasts touch very lightly in low flight
on soft wet grass, and pleasure seems to make
the flight itself into a sort of blue.
No whisper whispers through
the tall tree's top, although it always trembles.
Is not the flight around about my temples
weaving fresh garlands?

And do they not announce, all their brief cries,
some unknown benefit the heart perhaps
guesses, starting to hear it come that way?
They linger as their nests were out of mind,

34

and on the margin when they have flitted past
the rustle of their wings appears to stay.
The whole earth looks like clay
ready and offered for the work of love,
each cry a herald, and the dying eve
definitely day.

## Evening at Fiesole

My words to you in the evening freshen like
the rustle which those mulberry leaves are making
under his silent hand who still stands picking
them over, lingering since the work is slow
on his long ladder which is turning black
against the silvering bole,
the baring of the bough,
while our still unapparent Moon is spreading
beyond her sky-blue sill a delicate veil
illuming and illuding us;
almost it seems the countryside must feel
its flooding in her strange nocturnal chill,
its drinking in at every pore her peace,
while her it cannot see.

Now for your face, pale glittering like pearl, praise be,
O Evening, your huge eyes where heaven's water stays
silently still!

My words to you in the evening ought to bring
some gentleness like rainfall as it patters
down warmly till it scatters,
as 'twere the tearful valediction of the spring,
on the mulberries the elms and on the vines
and on the fresh and rosy fingers of the pines
playing upon the breeze till it is gone,
and on the grain still lacking its last pallor
but certainly not green,
and on the sickled hay which turns from yellow
to lose all colour,
and raining down on what Saint Francis loved to call
his brother olives turning hillsides pale
with rippling holiness.

Now you be praised for the fragrance of your dress,
O Evening, your horizon round you like the withy
holding the hay together!

I shall tell you towards what territories
of love we're summoned by the fabled River
whose sources in the shade of ancient trees
murmur the mountains' mystery for ever;
I shall tell what that secret is
which makes the hill-tops where they seem to hover
on clear horizons curve like lips that close
under some prohibition, while their will
to speak makes them so beautiful
beyond all our desire
whose silence can console
so that each evening they appear
less clear and yet more clear-
ly lovable.

Praised be your death because it is so very gradual,
O Evening, in the waiting which makes quiver
the earliest stars of all!

# The olive

Praise must rise to the olive in the morning!
And a garland that's simple, and a tunic
all of white, and a prayer that is sonorous
make up our feastday.

This tree's bright in the air and light and slender.
Why its brilliance should strike us all, however,
you or I have no means at all of telling,
more than the olive.

Narrow leaves, skinny branches, pocked and pitted
trunk, and roots like a scruffy beard, and very
tiny fruit – but uncomprehended godhead
gleams in that pallor!

Lady, know that the ancient Greeks commanded,
when the olive was planting or was picking,
chaste young men who were natives of the region
should have the office:

perfect chastity seemed the one essential
guardian good for a tree devote to Pallas
impure handling would spoil, the slightest breath of
misery wither.

You – who sleeping have passed right through the lustral
waters, walking without the least depression
over meadows of asphodel – come worthy
up to the olive.

And now vestured in white like figured Victory,
hair caught up all around your head, and pressing
on the glebe with your expeditious foot, you
come to the olive.

Breezes ripple across your flowing garments
where the billows are numerous like sea-spray
by the shore, and the olive twinkles at it
not having seen it.

Arms quite naked as Victory's own arms are,
up you're stretching upon your bending sandals,
reaching out for that branch, not overcrowded,
fit for a garland.

All we need is a simple wreath with slender
foliage: so that there is no weight or pressure
on our minds that are happy in the morning,
not the least shadow.

Come kind Light, like the air of early morning,
come like justice that's unobscured, in godlike
bareness come, with your gentle animation,
down on our spirits!

Touch those spirits as though they were the sacred
olive handled by you throughout its foliage;
nothing stay in our spirits unexamined
by you, All-seeing!

# The ear of corn

All praise at noonday to the ear of corn!
Inclining to the Sun which ripens her,
inclining to the earth where she was born,
she will bend more respectfully tomorrow
when she will finally be laid to rest
down with the tare her ill-intentioned brother,
with the oats growing wild
with cornflowers in light blue
with poppies blazing red
unsown by man, all in one sheaf together.

Her slender lines appear inviolate,
as though born only for admiring eyes;
her symmetry is such as breathes of power.
The grains are carefully distributed
along the lines, or folds, we recognize
from our great mother Vesta and her veil.
Three grains upon each rank;
the middle grain the smallest;
each with a separate husk;
each bristle springing out from its own scale.

All is not ripeness yet. The beard is green
still, at the point it rises from the scale,
although its prickly tip is all of gold.
There are green edges to the arid husk
in which the gradually hardening grain
turns to a flinty yellow more and more.
The upper stalk becomes
a pallid sort of green:
the lower stalk is white.
Beasts tramp and tramp to firm the threshing-floor.

The ancient says: 'In parts of the Maremma
already men begin to cut the grain.
And in some regions they have piled the stooks.
No one should start to reap until he sees
his harvest multitude, grown to one height,

gleaming in tawny redness all alike.'
And now the ear grows red.
The sickle's edge is bright;
the rest of the blade is dull
as stubble stalks burnt down to ashen black.

And first of all the sweaty hand, and then
the ear of corn will feel the cutting steel
against her stem; and yet the stem, its grain
still on it, will provide the candid flour
we need to make the pasta's mixture firm
and make the bread which rises as it bakes.
While the oats growing wild
the cornflowers in light blue
the poppies blazing red
fall to no purpose in the stubble stalks.

The hairy oats from yellow turn to white,
fashioned from light and fine and delicate;
the cornflower brings devoutly to our mind
the light blue eyes of Pallas our protectress;
the poppy's red resembles that young blood
which when the swordblade slashes gushes out;
and all are beautiful,
happily beautiful,
and harmless in their day:
and no man will go grieving for their fate.

And they'll be trodden down and from their sister
they were so happy to have growing near,
whom they heard sounding in the breeze – those beards
so many tiny lyres – be separated;
they will die unlamented as they're scattered
because they gave no bread to nourish man.
But they – oats growing wild
and cornflowers in light blue
and poppies blazing red –
should be commended like the ear of corn!

# Works and days

O venerable, married to the Earth,
how right we are each evening to review
the tasks of our tomorrow thoughtfully
and weigh our stamina with even hand.
Ancient, the words you speak come pouring down
like candid apple blossom at that time
when tiny fruit has just begun to set.
Speak to me; say what works you have in mind.
'In this month I prepare the threshing floor.
I clean it and when once it's lightly weeded
I dress it with a layer of chaff and dregs
to keep the harvest on it safe from rats
from emmets and from other harmful creatures.
And then I smooth it with a cylinder
of stone or wood; or else spread water on it
and on it loose the animals, so that
they trample and confirm it with their feet;
and then it dries in the sun' the ancient says.
He stands upon his threshold now repaired
with that stone which is said to be 'serene'
(much of it comes from Monte Cèceri)
a flawless stone, whose colour somewhat tends
to blue, almost the shade rainwater has
in which a leaf of dyer's woad is boiled.
And there behind his face – which his advanced
age has ploughed over with an unseen share
so that it radiates straight lines and curves,
a furrowed acre waiting for the seed –
there clambers up the doorpost out of stone
white jasmine always grateful to the bees,
a match in candour for his grizzled mane.
'In this month, at the summer solstice, when
the Sun can go no higher, then I sow
brassicas, which midway through August I
have to transplant to some well-watered place.
And beets and celery and coriander
and lettuce too I sow, and water them.
I also gather tares, and cut lucerne

42

for fodder. Then broad beans before it's light
I root up, in the waning moon; these beans,
even before the moon has finished waning,
I winnow; when they're aired I store them up.
In this month I must bud the peach and graft
the fig, and emptying out the hive I choose
the leader from the teeming swarm of bees.
And next there has to be the harvesting
of barley, which it's better if I should
complete before the ears begin to fall
or issue, since the grains are not protected
by clothing husks, as grains of wheat are clothed.
When I was young six bushels in one day
I used to reap!' So says the smiling ancient.
His gums are still well armed with teeth, as firm
when he is smiling as they are in speech.
His knees are steady too and never wobble,
although the sickle in its work has bent
his legs into the semblance of its own
curved steel. And on his venerable chest
rough linen indigo has almost turned
sky-blue makes him in some uncanny way
image great Pan ruler of all the stars,
upon whose breast is mirrored the whole Sky.

# The bard without a lyre

This ancient talks with me
about a kind of apple.
And says: 'It grows on a tree
of medium size, with blossoms that are white.
The sweetness of the fruit
is mixed with something tart.
Not unhappy with any soil, but found at best
in a climate that is mild, in soil that is rich.
It likes to be by the sea.
It shrinks from wind and frost.
It cannot be cross-bred.
Its season does not last.
The apples will keep in vessels smeared with pitch.
They also keep in shavings
of poplar-wood; or else, with dregs and grapeskins
in cauldrons they keep well a fair old time.'
The ancient reasons thus; in his sluggish speech
the heart has a higher reach,
above the Aonian mount.
An age-old rectitude is shining bright,
as in an early bard
singing some famous fate,
O Earth, in your witness with the hoary head.
The breath of his paternal
breast is the bounty of the very air
making the best of things.
The abundance of the life
of the tree is on a par
with the imposing destinies of kings.
He speaks, and between two bits
of wood weaves shining straw,
as though he were a bard stretching his strings,
created from the guts of little lambs,
between the arms of his lyre.
When the wind blows, there comes
a scent of clover from the shaded honey
strained out into the freshly-burnished vessels
after the hand has squeezed the loaded combs.

He reasons and he labours;
and the pale yellowish stalk remains unbroken.
From time to time he gazes
like one expecting signs.
He hears the swarm when it roars.
He speaks about the battles
the bees engage in in their very hives,
their lordship in the balance.
And there is shining in his beard and hair
a wisp or two of straw
nodding in time to his words.
There is no gold which shines so in the sun.
Hanging upon his lips which over-ripen,
catching the spicy flavour of his wisdom,
our soul is very like that wisp of straw.

# Beatitude

'Color of pearl her color, as befits
a ladye to display, not out of mesure.'
Is that your lady, Dante, in the figure
of humid Evening coming down to us?

Is it not Beatrice who from high heaven
comes down to us on earth,
her features drenched in love's recurrent dew?
With tears that never fail to trickle forth
she touches ears of corn
one at a time until they change their hue.
They look like people who,
finding themselves before her presence, kneel
down with bowed humble heads as if they feel
happy to meet the coming martyrdom.

Such silence overwhelms all animation.
In insubstantial circle
of hills, the pallid Arno is the sky.
The City is revealing very little
except two upright stems,
two towers, of prayer and of authority,
dear as to him they'd be,
her citizen before his banishment:
with something like a lily in his hand
he seemed to bow his head in scarlet folds.

Colour of pearl is spreading everywhere
in sky so very close
that every thought is nurtured like a wing.
All of the earth is loosened in the endless
smiling it had at heart,
and gradually it looks like vanishing,
the Angel worshipping
like this: 'Lorde, in this worlde of yours we see
a miracle in action, which proceeds
from a soule whose shining reaches to this highte.'

# Fvrit aestvs

A hawk's call clashes with the colour of pearl:
the sky is torn as one might tear a veil.
O shiver on the reticence of seas,
O breath, the index of the sudden squall!
O blood, my blood, so like the seas of summer!
The vital force entangles all the roots:
it lies below the earth, immense and hidden.
The stone shines more than any other torpor.

The light is covering such gulfs of silence,
like an immobile eye which hushes up
a rabid multitude of wild desires.
The Unknown comes, I wait for the Unknown!
That which was near me, look, it is now distant.
That which seemed living, look, it is extinguished.
I love you, cutting stone who on the rocky
ascent shine out to wound the naked foot.

My cruel thirst, to me you are more precious
than all the sweetest water of the streams.
Dwelling inside my turbulent peace is fever,
as there is fever dwelling in the marshes.
Chock-full of cries the recollected breast.
The hour is come, my Harvest, it is come!
Terrible in the midday, at its heart,
there weighs, O Harvest, your maturity.

# First dithyramb
ROMAE FRVGERIFAE DIC.

Where are the horses of the Sun
with their manes of fury and flame?
tails streaming out
and bound about
with bands of purple, their hooves
resplendent as they flash
on the parched ears of corn?
Where are the threshing-floors like circuses,
the threshing like a battle,
like athletes the country people?
Where are the horses of the Sun
loosed from their heavenly car?
Where the resounding whips,
the long reins left abandoned,
the jingling of the metal,
the glittering dripping backs?
Where are the shrieks, the songs, the dances?
Where is the lovely woman
covered with husks and bearded corn
like various golds and jewels?
Where are the scorns, the brawls,
the naked knives,
the blood which smokes and boils,
the stricken youth who falls
down into his own harvest
aspersed with his own rich blood
and his own vermilion wine?
Where is your godhead, Dionysus,
your laughter and your fury,
your peril?
Here is scanty harvest
for humble lives,
strait threshing-floor, light labour,
hands that are cautious, feeble throats.
O Maremme, coastal marshes,
pitiless beauty
born from Fever and Sun,

48

daytime kingdoms of Dis,
you are my dream!
O Rome, O Rome, the first
in the face of the Sun,
incombustible strength,
seed of glory,
sole offspring of the furrow
made by the violent man,
tall fertile ear of corn,
you are my dream and desire
in a wide sea of grain,
from solitary Cimino
to the vine-bearing hills of the Volsci,
as far as Minturno where wanders
old Mario's shade in the mire,
as far as Sinuessa
drunken with powerful Massic,
as far as the golden gates
of the promised Campania,
in a wide sea of grain
without number, O Rome,
as the races you lead in triumph
back from the battlefield!

First city of all the World,
as I was going away
from you, on the plain of Agro
I had a presage of blood
which inflamed me with newer
and even more vigorous love
for all of your altars
and for all of your tombs.
I saw a field of crimson
poppies stretched out in my sight
like a scene of carnage,
like a surge of blood still warm
disgorged from a hecatomb.
My wide eyes had never seen
such fervent red before,
and all my body was trembling

from its very roots
as if I were spilling my blood
on to your sacred soil
out of enormous veins.
And as I was going away,
impetuously
I turned around to look at you, inflamed
by the scalding grief
heard hissing like
a brand in an open wound;
and I was stretching towards
you, shouting your name
to the poppies' vermilion gleam
from the uproarious carriage
which bore me into exile.
And an intolerable ill
amongst all other ills
was my departure then;
life seemed so thin,
stripped of all strength and wings,
pallid, unable to rest,
bent over the bitter wound,
seeing itself so far away.

O Tuscany, O Tuscany,
dear for your orchards
the thorn encloses
the cypress guards;
dear for your hills
furrowed by rivulets
and garlanded by olives.
It was surely a rugged virtue
that placed together in your towers,
well-walled for civil war,
the sturdy stones;
and you are laden with great dead
in your sculptured sepulchres,
O Florence, city in flower,
lily of power,
Fiorenza, springtime shoot;

and certainly no gracefulness
exceeds your April grace
when all the valley is a cradle
of flowers of dreams of peace
and Simonetta in repose.
And yet the cradle for me
is the groove of the creaking carriage
on the stone of the Appian Way.
At the foot of Celio, unfrequented,
below the Porta Capena
I heard the trickling Acqua Marcia
slaking the burning City.
It moved among the tombs
and laurels, past Death which watches
and Glory which loses its leaves,
to the happy Alban Hills.
It left the pleasant shades behind;
no more did it see the long chain
of the aqueducts glow red;
it did not see fresh Preneste;
it scorned Tuscolo and its fruits,
Aricia and its woods which catch the light;
it rushed to the Tyrrhene shore
where raging storms endure
still but at their last gasp,
to Circe's gloomy halls
where Odysseus' keel struck land.
Longing for the waste land of light
where a vapour arises which poisons
when it seizes on wandering spirits,
it came to the candid rock
where Anxur appears to float
in grim dogdays, hanging over
the death-bearing pool and the Sea.

Path to the sun, O Appian Way,
in the face of blazing wind from the South,
Appian Way, from the Porta Capena
whose hidden spring
murmurs assiduous drops,

where will you lead me,
the soul of impatience
and blazing with greed?
It is not here that my harvest is reaped.
To reap my lofty harvest
a thousand tireless scythes
worked furrow after furrow,
from dawn to sunset,
through nine dawns
and through nine sunsets
in a land up to then unknown.
And at every noon we heard
coming from the horizon
in flames the voice
and the thunder of Pan upon us.
And the ferocious crowd was howling:
'O Pan, help us, help us!'
And throughout the stubble the candid
oxen, yoked to the carts
up against the broken stooks,
were bellowing over again.

O Pan, give me my grain,
give me the gold of my southern
harvest and the frenzy of Lybian
south winds and the frenzy of horses'
hooves resplendent with lightning flashes!
It was not here, not here, that I had my fields,
not here I had my carts,
but on wide Lazio's Tyrrhene edge,
as far as Minturno,
as far as Sinuessa,
in the region drunken with Massic,
in the region drunken with Caecuban,
to lacustrial Fondi,
to coastal Amicle,
to Danaean Ardea
where the blood of Turnus burns,
and on the curved shore which is named
after Aeneas's nurse,

this side of rapacious Volturno,
and near to the silent pool
rich in reeds and sea-lettuce
where Latinus's laurel flourishes
among the embrowning ears,
and to Anzio, dear to the pirate,
and dear to merciless Fortune
and to the merciless Emperor,
and to Ostia, sacred mouth
of the Tiber bristling with prows
and swollen with sails,
where long granaries crowd.

I scythed and threshed on every side
at wide Lazio's Tyrrhene edge,
to the City's gates, to the farthest
border, between Tiber and Liri,
in all the most fertile tracts.
But my sighs are drawn to you,
to you, shadow of Monte Circèo
bearing death like the poison
and the charm of the greedy witch
who held the insomniac
pilot-king of Ithaca, Odysseus,
in the bed with the towering columns.
There still reigns on the Mountain
the shrewd Goddess, daughter of the Sun;
she keeps watch from her rocky palace
among her spangled panthers
and her cups with their poisoned juice.
Her imprisoned lovers groan,
the brutes of her pleasure;
she touches their foreheads
with a wand and whispers some words.
And her herdsmen with their lances, the issue
of the Bacchante and the Centaur,
engendered in the gadfly's panic hour,
with hides of bronze, with sorrel coats,
in a rage and a frenzy,
hurl there their hoarse

howls on to the marsh
and goad the black herd
with hairless tails –
the buffaloes, angry monsters
sunk and stretched out in the muddy
pasture concealed in a wood of horns.
And, when day comes,
all of the marsh is puffing and panting
through the just-emerging nostrils and jaws,
and it looks with a thousand ghastly eyes;
and the putrid water gurgles
and boils, impeded by the grasses
the parted hoof uproots,
while a sinister cloud of crows
darkens and deafens the air
where Fever veiled in a haze
passes in deadly silence.

I shall do my threshing there,
there I shall thresh my harvest
on a threshing-floor as vast
as the field where a host is drawn up.
Where are the horses of the Sun
with their manes of fury and flame?
tails streaming out
and bound about
with bands of purple, their hooves
resplendent as they flash
on the parched ears of corn?
Where the resounding whips,
the long reins left abandoned,
the jingling of the metal,
the glittering dripping backs?
Where are the shrieks, the songs, the dances?

And here at the festival are the horses!
Who is guiding them?
Here are the whips, and the rattles,
the hollow-sounding cymbals
overgone by the beating of hearts,
the women barefoot and girded up

drunken with light,
young men with the strength of bulls
drunken with noise.
The flower of the Latin race.
The wineskins swollen with wine.
The must it is sweet to mix.
The dry bread giving us thirst.
Here is the cup of clay,
of antique style and ancient beauty,
huge as the skull of an ox,
and pink as a breast.
All that belongs to a festival!
Pour out the sheaves
on the vulcanic soil,
pour them out of the leaning
cart, sheaves
from a cornucopia.
All the earth seems redder
to eyes that are blurred
than sinopia is.
The wind is whirling,
raising the eddying dust.
On to the threshing-floor the carts
are pouring the stridulous gold.
The gold mounts up.
The igneous soil disappears
beneath the mass
of innumerable ears.
The whole wide surface becomes
one single sheaf, one aureate mountain.
The whole of Lazio is a field of stubble
burning and sinking into ash,
from Sinuessa famed for its Massic
to the city of Romulus, Rome.
The whole wide surface becomes
one single sheaf, one aureate mountain;
and the horses are climbing on to it.
Tread it down, tread it down!
O Rome, this is the mountain of Ceres,
the mother of Proserpine,

the mountain of Cybele, the Great Mother
who sailed on the Tiber.
The terrible horses
prancing on solid hooves
are climbing it in their assault.
Tread it down, tread it down!
The sheaves are shaken about
under the shock, the stalks
are broken, the ears
are threshed from their husks, beards rustle,
the chaff flies.
Tread it down, tread it down!
The whips crack,
and flicker in the air
like lightning flashes.
Like the hawsers
of a perilous ship
in a squall,
the reins are stretched tight.
Human pulses throb,
muscles quiver,
arteries swell.
Who has the boldness to govern
the strength of the Winged Hooves?
They bound, these beasts,
they prance, they beat
the air, and with their fourfold iron
they shatter the mounds.
Tails arch themselves untrimmed,
manes flutter
like vivid banners,
nostrils breathe
out flame, eyes are striated
with blood, flanks throb,
veins stand out,
down the wide backs sweat
is running in streams,
in the foam of the difficult bits
the rainbow shines.
Tread it down, tread it down!

All of the fire of the bestial
souls, exhaled
in the panting rush,
seems to surround
the dripping bitter bodies,
and trembles over the sweat
like an invisible wing.
Does there rise in these rapid
hearts the craving of Pegasus
for the sidereal road?
Tread it down, tread it down!
The wind is whirling,
stirring up into scarcely substantial
clouds the spoils of the grain.
The air is alive with volatile
gold, through which these candid
and black and sorrel
and maculate backs are shining,
and which is shot through
with hoarse shouts,
the cracking of whips, the hisses,
the clash of the rattles,
the ring of the cymbals,
the bellowing of the buffaloes,
the laugh of the women
whom Liber knows how to arouse.

But the sky is spreading out,
silent and solemn, over the festival;
the distant Lower Sea is calm
where the son of Venus
from the high Ilian prow
shouted: 'Italy! Italy!'
And the shade of the king of Ithaca,
the shade of the ancient sailor,
the expert on men and seas,
looks out from the magic
rock to see if his iron Fate
calls him once more to subdue
some greater peril.

57

O Power, Abundance, Victory,
the terrestrial task is under
your auspices, witnessed by you!
Great Lazio is all
lit up by you. The light
of day goes purple.
The wind stops whirling.
The air strikes into the earth.
In all things there seems to be born
unutterable life,
for the early Italic gods
return of a sudden
from the Original Shade
to live again in the glebe,
in the water in the grass in the flint,
and over there, within the palace
of King Latinus the son
of Marica and of Faunus,
the Laurel grows green again
which was sacred to Phoebus
Apollo before Creusa's
widower came
from Ilium to be joined
with the fruitful maiden Lavinia.
O miracle! O metamorphosis!
On the wide surface,
square like the Saturnian
City at its foundation,
the trampled harvest like the western
cloud is empurpled.
Tread it down, tread it down!
And the horses are shining
pink, as if in the depths
of their blood a sudden
dawn were lit up
and through the smoky
flanks were seen to transpire.
They rise with a rosy fire
round their breasts and bellies,
where the swelling veins

interlace like ivy's
entanglement on the bark.
Spirit of flame
breathes from their nostrils.
Tread it down, tread it down!
Now men perceive
that a godlike rhythm
is controlling the rush
of these beasts with their solid hooves.
O miracle! O metamorphosis!
Look, the Titanian wings,
the sunlike vans, the lightbearing
feathers, untiring
scourges of the diurnal
Ether, engines
of the most precipitate speed,
which the web of muscle
seemed to hold close
against hard shoulder-blades,
look, look, they are freeing themselves
unfolding and spreading.
In the gold in the purple
the extended wings
are throbbing, the Apollonian wings.
The wind which they raise
lifts up the hearts of men
like a paean sung
through sacred colonnades
to a myriad lyres.
Io Paean! Io Paean! Glory
to the Lord of the Works,
to the Mirror of Men,
to the Titan with sparkling locks,
to the King of wingèd words,
to the Leader of Helicon's dances!
O Power, Abundance, Victory,
and you, Rome's Genius never subdued,
be witnesses to me here.
The horses of the Sun are treading
the reborn grain of Rome.

# Peace

Silence, silence! The beautiful Simonetta
embellished with the lily of a day
wanders without an escort on the fa-
ding banks and sings a novel ballatetta.

The hills are curving, curving very slightly,
like waves the wind has blown in ocean sand,
casting, as they were made of air, no shadow.
The Arno prattles, rattles the white gravel,
and bears to the Tyrrhenian Nereids
that veil the Grace washed in the Arno's waters,
the very veil perhaps
in which she wraps this country of Toscana,
long left the homely woollen trade behind her,
of arts one time her prime.
Silence, silence! Now summon back your rhyme
into your heart, a bee in skep again.
And hear the tenzon now, this end of June,
cicada and skylark sing in mild vendetta!

# The tenzon

O Marina di Pisa, when the sun in Leo
dazzles the dogdays!
Skylarks are singing up above the meadows
of San Rossore,
cicadas in the planetrees on the Arno,
singing a tenzon.

As Summer lives with gold inside her mouth,
the Arno carries silence to its mouth.
All of the morning through the pleasant plain
singing from this side, other singing there,
water in silence in between two voices.
Now Summer leans from one side of the boat
and now upon the other bends to listen.
Slowly the river, but the boat moves swiftly.
The bank is growing fresh and like a garland.
You smile continually with shining mouth,
like Summer smiling on me, shining Summer!
Always above us are the boat's white sails,
above us the immaculate white sails.
The wind, while it is touching
on them, touches upon your tired eyelids,
and touches too your smooth and sensitive veins;
a godlike drowsiness is breathing through you,
fresh on your eyelashes as are the dews
on herbage in the dawn.
Your blood is turning azure like the ocean.
Your soul is garlanded about with peace.
The Arno carries silence to its mouth,
as Summer lives with gold inside her mouth.
Flock upon flock of birds across the mouth,
then all those wings are bathing in the ocean!
All my past harm falls into disregard.
All vain desires are quenched, all wild desires.
What hurt me yesterday, hurts me no longer;
and that which touched me once, no longer touches.
And in my heart every demand is calm,
water in silence in between two voices.

So I travel to the ocean;
and so I sail. Over the pleasant plain
singing from this side, other singing there.

Skylarks are singing up above the meadows
of San Rossore,
cicadas in the planetrees on the Arno,
singing a tenzon.

# Mouth of the Arno

Simply no woman's mouth for me had ever
such smoothness all my amorous career
(except for yours, except for yours, now here)
as this, the colourless and silent mouth
of the little stream that springs in Falterona.
What woman can surrender
(except for you, except for you) as gently
as this wide current when it settles down?
It does of course not sing,
but like a melody it presses on
to where salt is.

    I hardly hope to express
    what its great charm may be,
    like one who, sleeping, hears
    sounds he can't recognize,
    and sleeps away.

Green waves are bounding up against the river,
billow on foaming billow,
waves like young animals, such grace and fervour.
Not even Donatello
put into dancing children so much pleasure,
the marble foaming underneath his chisel,
to decorate the white cathedral choirs.
Under such garlands of such fruit such flowers
the dance developed all around the pulpits
of lines of children, yet not such a dance
as this of dancing waves.

    Is there creature which lives
    in so much grace,
    and in such pure
    pleasure, unless that skylark there
    which strides about in space?

There is my soul perhaps, whenever it loses
itself inside its song, and sees the glory;

there is your soul perhaps, whenever it loses
itself in love and loses all the memory
of fleeting illusions where it was entrammelled;
both of us eager for high victory.
And maybe we shall get a grasp of all
the happiness of the free
billows, and of the strong expanded wings,
and of the savage hymn without restraint.
Worship and wait!

Worship, worship, and wait!
You see? Your naked feet
leave tracks of liquid light,
and wonders rise before your eyes
out of the water. See?

Great calyxes are growing from the water
in open-work of finest golden thread.
The clouds the woods the mountains shores and water
are visible behind those giant flowers
and unattainable
as foreign countries in a dreaming head.
Butterflies, golden, like your hands, in pairs
are fluttering to discover on the water
the huge exotic blooms in some alarm,
while you are breathing in
the salty smell.

The sunlit Hour
is playing in godlike fun,
in colour variable
as, when it sings and stretches out,
a dove is at the throat.

They are the hanging nets. Some are suspended,
as they were balances, from long antennae
fixed upon high projecting landing-stages
where someone waits to raise or lower the line,
and others from the bows of pinnaces
which slip across a mirror

always refracting them; and when the sun
is striking on the stern, and when the oar
is held at rest, a radiance alters them:
great calyxes are growing from the water,
lilies of fire.

   Meanwhile the youthful Hour
   is playing in godlike fun,
   that hour which is as short
   as song of dove. Enjoy the charm,
   our soul, and worship it!

## Between two Arnos

This is Procne's isle
where you smile
at the cries
of the swallow from Thrace
who along the soft clays
makes and remakes
her age-old rebukes
to the king of deceits,
and without pause or peace,
as soon as day dawns,
goes and returns
making her nest
with zest,
nor pauses for rest
until there is cover
of shade on the river
near night,
on the isle which moves light
with reeds in wet clay,
giving the flautist
his flute,
the migrant her nest,
and maybe the best
of beds for our love if you smile.
This is the gentle isle.

This is the gentle isle
between two Arnos,
the cradle of song,
where all Summer long
the verdant reeds
respond to the breeze
in varying modes,
don't you hear?,
as if they were clear
of knots and of pith,
and inspired by the breath
of changeable lips

and touched with the tips
of skilful fingers,
elected with art
god-given,
and bound
in groups,
with linen
and wax wound round,
tasting of honey,
seven by seven,
reed-pipes made
in perfect style.
This is Procne's isle.

# The rain in the pine wood

Sh! Here on the sill
of the wood I can't hear
any human
words you might say; but I hear
less usual
words of the drops on the leaves
far away.
Just hear. There is rain
from the clouds which are rare.
On the tamarisks rain –
they are salty and scorched –
rain on the pines
with their scales and bristles,
rain on the myrtles
which are sacred to Venus,
rain on the brooms which gleam
with clustering flowers,
on the junipers thick
with scented berries,
rain on our faces,
our sylvan faces,
rain on our hands
which are bare,
our clothes
which are sheer,
on the new thought
the freshened soul
puts out,
on the fine fable
which yesterday
deluded you, today deluding me,
O Ermione.

D'you hear? There is rain
on a solitude
of green,
a rustle going on
which changes in the air,

changes as the leaves
are more or less rare.
Listen. What we hear respond
to the plaint of the rain is the sound
of cicadas
no southern lament
can terrify,
nor the ashen sky.
And the pine
has a sound of its own,
and myrtle and juniper
others again – all instruments,
no two the same,
under numberless fingers.
We are sinking here
in the atmosphere
of the wood,
living arboreal life:
your elated face
is wet with the rain
like a leaf,
and your locks
are fragrant as
bright junipers,
O you creature of earth
whose name
is Ermione.

Listen, listen. The tune
from the airy cicadas
little by little
is being toned down
beneath the lament
which is growing more loud as
a song joins in
which is hoarser,
which arises from yonder
shade which is damp and remote.
More muffled, more faint,
it slackens, it's spent.

Only one note
still trembles, until it dies out,
and rises, and trembles, dies out.
The voice of the sea is not heard.
But over the frond
the splashing is heard
of the silver rain
which is clean,
a splashing which varies
as the frond
is denser, less dense.
Listen.
The child of the air
is dumb; but the child
of the mud in the distance,
the frog,
sings in the depth of the shade,
who knows where, who knows where!
And it rains on your eyelashes here,
Ermione.

It rains on your black
lashes: it seems you weep
but with pleasure; not white,
but almost as if you were green,
you seem to appear out of bark.
And everything in us is fresh
and scented,
the heart in the breast like a peach
unspoilt by touch,
in the shade of their lids the eyes
are pools of water in grass,
the teeth in their gums
white as almonds before they are ripe.
And we're walking from bush to brake,
now joined and now apart
(and the rough green vigour
ties up our ankles,
entangles our knees)
who knows where, who knows where!

And there is rain on our faces,
our sylvan faces,
rain on our hands
which are bare,
our clothes
which are sheer,
on the new thought
the freshened soul
puts out,
on the fine fable
which yesterday
deluded me, today deluding you,
O Ermione.

## The roots of song

My words are children born
of the forest,
of the wave,
of the sand,
of the Sun,
of the wind from the west.
My words
are as profound
as roots
in the ground,
sometimes serene
as the firmament,
as hot as the hot vein
of the adolescent,
bristling as brambles
bristle, as obscure
as smoke which rambles,
as clear
as rock-crystal,
as leaves of the poplar
tremulous,
as swollen as the nostril
of the horse
which gallops ahead,
as fleeting as perfumes
which gradually spread,
as fresh as calyxes
just opened wide,
as cool as the dew
of nocturnal skies,
as gloomy as asphodel
on Hades' field,
bending as willows bend
over a pond,
as delicate as the strand
running from stalk to stalk
which a spider has unwound.

# The name

Lady, this name of yours
was the name of a city with walls
in Argolis, land of dust.
And in that land there was,
they say, such a short path
to go down into hungry
Hades, into the jaws
of death, that the citizens
left out of the dead mouth
the customary fare
for the infernal ferry,
the sombre obolus
for the boatman of the Styx.
Also this name of yours
belonged to the daughter of famous
Helen, the candid flower
of Sparta, of Leda's blood,
illustrious as gold,
to the daughter born of her
who shone upon the earth
as though an extra Season
of endless joys and pleasures,
the torch and glass of Venus,
wound of the champion.
Ermione, Ermione
with voice spring-water-clear
tending at times to green
like water in the shade
of maidenhair, with eyes
fostered alike by beauty
and freshness, eyes twin-born,
eyes children of the Grace
and children of the Dream,
dear to the poet, skilled
to weave a living garland
and praise for your abundant
poet who satisfies
with untamed melodies,

73

to me your name is sweet
always as clustered fruit,
or that hoarse rustic flute,
the evening thickets hear,
a cluster of black grapes
is the sweetness of your name,
the crocus when in flower,
or in July fresh rain.

# Before dawn

You walking on the barren shore
will gather more
and more nocturnal melodies,
gather the lily of a day,
making yourself fresh coronals,
while down to black abysses borne
the Pleiades,
grandchildren of old Ocean, wester,
still weeping for their brother Hyas
the tender lioness has torn.

We shall walk silent on the shore,
and feel upon ourselves the dew,
the clean pure dew,
rain from the dilatory eyes
of night-time almost at death's door,
while where the sky has almost cleared
the Pleiades,
grandchildren of old Ocean, wester,
under the menace of the cruel
huntsman Orion and his sword.

And I alone shall turn my face,
looking where we have walked, and see
the luminous and liquid trace
your feet leave there;
in silence we shall stand and listen,
while down in dreadful grief and fear
the Pleiades,
grandchildren of old Ocean, wester,
and Dawn with her white veil is drying
the lamentation of their eyes.

# The two eyes of a Pleiad

In your pupil now,
in the round
of the golden eye,
there is the prow,
the pointed prow
of the ancient vessel,
as it can be seen
in the Thessalian coin,
shining,
as in the astound-
ing coins of power
upon the sea,
as in the stater
from the port in Lycia
the pirates from Phoenicia
called Phaselis.
The wind is with us!

And in the other pupil
there glitters
the ear of corn, a flame,
as in the tetradrachm
from Leontini
on the River Lyssus
the wealth of Sicily,
the godlike grain.
And, if I look steadily
at you, the two kinds of art
take my heart apart.
O hard soil split!
Long furrow on the sea!
And in both places
there is refuge for my mind,
O my Pleiad
of the sea and the land.

# The tributaries

This is the river-mouth
that today is the colour of honey,
and gentle so that Love
is holding it to your lips
like a cup that is brimming over.
I have praised it with my art.
But how very many waters
flow into this one water,
with such rapacious force
into, O Fluviale, this slow peace!

And it is not given to us
to empty the brimming cup,
distinguishing those flavours.
Who now will praise Ombrone
seen by Lorenzo once
bursting out of his grotto
hard on the heels of Ambra?
Again he calls to the Arno:
'You are my only hope.
Help quickly, lest the flying nymph escape.'

Who will praise the Bisenzio
so precious to that ancient
elegant fabulist
who praised the perfect beauty
of the lady who was perfect?
The Pescia and the Era?
The Pesa and the Elsa?
The Greve and the Sieve?
Who will praise the cool soft rills
which drop from the Casentino's verdant hills?

Fresh uproar in among
smooth polished stones, bright clays,
banks grown with grasses, rows
of lofty poplars, ponds
surrounded by young willows,

dark hollows full of fish,
shades where the golden quarrel
is striking, twists and turns,
which of you now enjoys
himself, creating in his heart your praise?

This is the mouth; how much
land running water covers,
not to be seen unmoved!
Valleys are hollowed out
like the hand of one who drinks;
mountains are swollen like
a woman's breast unpressed.
The flock crosses the ford.
The millwheel sounds like thunder.
One spring is solitary in Falterona.

The evening falls. The moon
rises on rocky La Verna,
the moon, a rosy nimbus
for him who pours out peace
without a word being said.
Peace holds the mountain ranges.
Pratomagno's long spine
seems to become more smooth
as though beneath the bland
sleepy persuasion of a friendly hand.

Over the wooded plains
the charcoal-kilns are burning
like ceremonial fires.
The Arno gleams through poplars.
At every breath of wind
loud rustles drown the choral
lament of the wingèd flutes
the creeping couch-grass hides.
No other voice, no sound.
The water runs from the mountains to this mouth.

# The camels

Our beach at Pisa, this
beach loved by all our race,
of living sand and water,
with woods the length of the shore,
O strong and sure creation,
in which there takes delight
nature's untiring art
which never fails or trembles,
earth delicate and strong
as though it were outlined
by the ever-certain hand
of the potter whence is born
that vase which is most precious
although it does not glitter
or weigh a ton, pure form,
pride of the dining-table
and of the Etruscan tomb,
the flower of every form
in art's unaltering sky –
I ask by what weird chance
there reached us from immense
Asia or over-dry
Africa this ungainly
pack-animal so plainly
leaving its printed tracks
upon your fine warm sand,
and why, like the beast that is maned
and friendly to humankind,
this monster should be seen
carrying on its hump
spoils of the wood between
the Arno and the Sea?

They pass among the bushes
and make their way to the shore
between the timber-dumps,
between the piles of brushwood,
these camels with their humps

loaded with heavy bundles
of loppings and of straw,
solemn silent and sad!
Beneath their twisted feet
dry pinecones and dead needles
rustle and grate and creak.
The jackdaw is turning about
in a sky that is choked with heat;
occasionally it crows.
Sweet-smelling resin flows.
And on the Hollows Beyond
there comes to us a sound
of neighing now and again;
and a slighter kind of whinny,
a much less certain kind,
is heard, more fresh, in answer,
from colts just newly born.
The sad and solemn camels
are passing through the bushes.
And now it is not their Berber
who guides them, but the Tuscan
peasant with age-old words
his fathers used before him
along the labouring furrow
encouraging the oxen
when they were slow to work.
They stir their calloused hides.

They come at last to the clearing
to lay their burdens down.
All of a sudden it seems
that the reason why they squat
is to breathe their very last
and rot upon the spot.
They're bending at the knees
emitting a low cry.
They yawn then in the sun.
Rough yellow teeth are seen
in rows, and violet
palates. We notice, rising

the length of their serpentining
and hairy woolly throats,
an intermittent gurgle.
Their flaccid lips are trembling,
they're weeping out of brown
exhausted eyes, dead mirrors
of desert tracts and groves
of palmtrees. They seem older
than this old World itself,
these archetypal exiles,
exhausted and oppressed
by all the tiredness
afflicting living flesh
across the troubled face
of this discordant Earth.
They rise without their loads.
From their bare sides the cords
hang down at length and trail
along the path. We hear
their melancholy gurgle.

Perhaps they looked like this
upon their native shores.
That merchant out of Pisa
regarded them with horror;
he had been caught and taken
prisoner by the corsairs
and carried far from home.
As bad luck had to have it
he fell in with a pirate
galley from Barbary,
well armed with twenty-two
oars on each side, and strong
and rapid as an arrow.
He lost to thieving hands
just everything he had,
his galleon with square sails
and all his merchandise.
And he was thrown in bonds.
For long years he remained

a slave in Barbary.
He ground the grain by hand,
hearing from time to time
a hollow futile cry
come from the stricken camel
beaten and sick to death.
Then, ransomed, he returned
to Pisa and his estates.
He made himself a new
mansion the Arno mirrored.
Mindful of servitude
he wrote above the door
these words: FROM HAND TO MOUTH.

And loved the Arno the more.

# Noon

In the middle of the day
upon the Etruscan Sea –
a sort of pallid green
like bronzes we exhume
from hypogea – the calm
is heavy. Not a breath
of wind is blown.
Not a reed trembles
upon the lonely shore
rough with butcher's-broom
and scorching juniper. No sound
of voices, if I listen.
The line of sails becalmed
towards Livorno
looks white. Through the bright
silence I can see
Cape Crow and the Island of the Light-
house; and not so near
airy forms in the air –
the islands which expressed your anger,
Dante our master –
Capraia and Gorgona.
Marmoreal crown
of menacing peaks,
the great Apuan Alps
rear up in pride
and lord it over the salt realm.

The mouth – a lake
of salt and coloured like
sea seen through stilted huts,
and through enormous nets
hanging from poles and struts
arranged like crosses – is quite still.
Like the sepulchral bronze
of pallid green, the smile
is tranquil on this mouth.
Almost lethean,

oblivious, still,
it shows no sign
of a current, no wrinkle
raised by a breeze. The two banks
merge in the distance
as in a circle
of reeds, wrapped round
by calm oblivion; from the reeds
no rustle. Deeper green,
the woods of San Rossore
stand darkly round;
but the more distant woods,
towards Gombo, towards the Serchio,
are almost blue.
The Pisan Hills are asleep
covered by crowds
of motionless clouds.

Calm and heat
and silence everywhere.
Summer is ripening
over my head like a fruit
promised to me,
which I must gather
with my own hand,
which I must suck
with my own lips.
All traces of men
are lost. No sound
of voices, if I listen. Human pain
has gone.
I no longer have a name.
And I feel my face
turn golden in the gold
of noon,
and I feel my fair
beard shine
like ocean straw;
I feel the beach which is ruled
in lines by the delicate

work of the waves
and winds is like
my palate, is like
the hollow of my hand
where touch is most refined.

And my strength stretched on the ground
is stamped into the sand
and spread into the sea;
and the river is my blood,
the hill is my forehead,
the wood is my pubis,
the cloud is my sweat.
And I am in the flower
of the rush, in the scale
of the pinecone, in the juniper
berry, in tangle,
in ocean straw,
in everything exiguous,
in everything huge,
in the sand which is contiguous,
in the distant range.
I burn, I shine.
And I no longer have a name.
And the alps and the islands and the gulfs
and the capes lighthouses woods
and the mouths which I have named
have lost their usual names
sounded on human lips.
I no longer have a name or fate
among men; Noon
is how I am known. I live in everything,
tacit as Death.

And my life is divine.

# The mothers

On the Hollows Beyond,
in the salty straw,
in the brown reed-beds,
in the yellow grasses,
lounge in their herds
the sorrel and bay
horses
of San Rossore.
Some on the sand-
banks, others immersed
in water up to their bellies,
they nuzzle each other's noses;
their backs shine
in the sun,
bright, dark, golden, copper.
On these Hollows, where ducks
shelter in winter,
they lounge in the light
in their fertility,
their pregnant flanks
a motionless mass
of peace. Only
over shallow water
their long tails
wave steadily
from side to side. There is
from time to time
from the wet
nostrils a shudder, a snorting,
a light panting,
an uncertain whinny,
in the silent river mouth;
from the shore in reply
comes the feeble undertow
of the sea. One of them
comes out from the herd, sniffs
at the water, and slowly drinks;
then she stares at the mountain

where a smoky cloud
is gathering;
then she turns about to nuzzle again.
And the tails are waving
slowly above the repose
of the fertile herd.
Together with you, pure Light,
together with you the Mothers
in peace expect
the birth.

In the distance through bright air
massive and shapely
sky-blue and white
the Alps of Carrara appear,
sky-blue with shade
and white with quarries.
But silent cloud
gathers to clutter
the peaks
where lightnings
and eagles nest.
A sharp scent from the distance,
from pines that are yellow and green,
and borne upon
rare breaths of wind, reaches
this calm place.
And look, there is a ship,
Etruscan sails
coming from the shore
of crescent Luni
snowy with marble.
There is a ship in sight
between the Serchio and Gombo.
It is loaded with blocks of marble,
loaded with dreams
which sleep in the deep
candour alone and unknown.
And my spirit calls up
your mad Evangelist,

O Buonarrotti,
the son of the Earth
kindled by Genius;
I see the great body
twist in the torture
of the restricting block,
whence with an effort
the rough knee breaks free, and the thigh
huge with its muscle and bone.
In the ship's hold sleeps
the fecund freight
of forms, drawn out
of remote quarries,
snatched from the lap of the Alps.
In the lap of the ship
the white masses sleep.
From lonely dreams the Mothers
expect
the birth.

# Calm

O wedding morning
between the Pisan Sea
and the Alps of Luni!
O wedding unlimited in space
and brief in time!
The beautiful cloud
is wed
to the hill which rises towards her,
the shadow of both weds the plain,
the fresh water weds the salt,
the reed the branch of the vine,
the willow
the flowering rush,
the capstan the fishing-net
on the mouth of the river teeming with fish,
my rhyme my joy,
the seaweedy
sand your gentle feet,
O Ermione.

And the sky is snowy
as upon your rippling cheek
the unaccustomed
veil.
The sea is of opal
with chrysolite veins,
like Asian seas'
unmoving brightness
of molten gems.
Jellyfish are bright
upon the flat
of the emergent bank.
And everything is white,
near and far.
There is great calm
from shore to shore,
as when on the Sea of Sicily
she builds her nest –
the bride Alcỳone.

# The highest Alps

Ermione, awake,
out of your bed of sea-lettuce,
O lady of the shores.
Gaze at a novel sight,
the Gods appearing
on the Alps of Luni,
on the highest height!
Actually western clouds, but rather like
a crown, death-struck,
on every everlasting peak.
What this resembles most is a great
and solemn assembly
of godheads meeting and greeting
from Sagro to Giovo,
from Pania to Tambura,
with the tawny eagle
of the Thunderer
spreading its feathers
over each sacred seat.
O Tyrrhenian silences
on the waste Gombo!
Pure solitude,
untracked!
Candour of distant blocks of marble,
of statues not yet born,
the finest!
The Pisan Hills are asleep,
weighed down
in leaden blue,
upon the sleeping plain.
A different race of hills.
They have no divinity, no tutelary gods,
nor in their caves haruspices,
no impulses of zeal
for sunsets,
no madness, no pain;
but they are asleep
upon the sleeping plain.

O Alps of Luni,
finest of all things face
to face with the Sea,
rock which will last into ages,
O Sign which the spirit discerns,
terrestrial yearning
towards the Master
Creator,
Promethean matter,
unsleeping altitude,
with wings to fly,
Hymn with no words,
flesh of bright statues,
glory of lasting temples,
strength of the raised
columns,
substance of forms
which never decay!

## Gombo

The immensity of grief,
of mourning without cure and with
no end, turned into earth
like Niobe to weeping rock,
seems to be dwelling there
on the deserted shore, in sheer
alps, and within the wood
making its aromatic wail.

There all is high and pure,
and dismal like that other world
where all through Time persist
the stringent punishments inflicted
by rigour of the gods
on men oblivious that sacred
limits have been imposed
on their desire to be immortal.

The Mystery of the World
has spoken three immense words here,
through Sea through Shore through Alps,
one godlike visible enigma
enrapturing with fear
and ecstasy the human soul
tormented with the body's
weight and the energy of wings.

Since all the strength of Life
could never comprehend so much
beauty, then here is Death
possessing arms that are more vast
silences more intent
rapidity that is more sure;
yes here is Death, and Art
who is her everlasting sister:

yes she who even seizes
on Life and rescues it for ever

from all the toils of Time
and lifts it sheer between the Shade
and Light, and gives to it
a fresher breath a livelier rhythm:
so Death and Art appear
to me within the fatal circle.

O Niobe, I hear
your sudden ancient cry ring out
along the sounding Sea,
and your despairing agony
calling your sons and daughters
throughout the inexorable circle,
and hear the powerful bow
creak and I hear the arrow whistle.

Thera, Phtia, Cleossa,
Astioche, and Phaedimos:
such were the names you called.
Those names, as smooth and sweet as honey
within your mouth, O Mother,
were fractured into savage howling
as by the missive gold
your children's bloom of youth was broken.

They fall upon their breasts
and sides, in all the flower of youth
they fall, the very handsome
young men, the very gentle maidens;
they cover the salt sand;
their hair is matted, but with foam
and not with gore, the wound
being bloodless from this lethal gold.

They fall down to remain
about your feet, demented Mother!
Then all is marble and
silence itself an effigy.
The immensity of grief
is made terrestrial and marine.

The Sea the Shore the Alps
are your funereal shade your image.

Niobe, over-bold,
I see the beauty of your face
petrified with your plaint
across this bloodless solitude,
the sacrilegious pride
which made you look around for altars
devoted to your power
of giving life, your mortal womb.

All there is high and pure
gloomy and challenging the skies,
mindful of all-too human
greatness and punishment of gods.
And in no other region
is the audacious soul, alas,
so troubled by this weight
of body and this work of wings.

# Orphic anniversary

P.B.S.
VIII JULY MDCCCXXII

We heard on the waste Gombo in a dream
Triton's enormous twisted trumpet blown where
Luni was echoing the sonic boom
to Populonia.

We heard the whole of Mare Nostrum shake,
from hoary breakers to where sea-gulfs twist,
as when it's whipped to frenzy by the great
wings of the East.

I started: 'Lady, do you know what this is?
What proclamation through the shell's inspired?
Does it bring back to us from salt abysses
the severed head?

The bloodless head of Orpheus, the Thracian
carried by Bacchic fury quite away
down the cold Hebrus, reaching through the Aegean
the Etruscan Sea?'

The evening like a forge was burning dark;
and in the highest height the eagles cried;
the Apuan outline shone enamel-like
a rosy red.

Imagined pouring out of broken urns,
the rivers seemed to roar in that flushed circle,
the Arno where wild Dante haunted once,
the Magra, the Serchio.

She said: 'It is not Thracian Orpheus,
not lyre and severed head still sweeping on;
but he who gave himself in sacrifice
up to the Storm.

This is the day he died. Our castaway,
who left the Angles as a fugitive,
is coming back, who loved Antigone,
and loved the olive.'

I said: 'You are clear-sighted: how should we
celebrate his arrival on the shore?
Shall we invoke the Heroes' company?
I hardly dare.

Our castaway may come with eyes wide open
bearing the image of a world that he
cannot express but saw in the uncertain
depths of the sea.

He who had snatched Prometheus from the vulture,
and in the very bosom of Causation
roused out of sleep the aboriginal monster
Called Demogorgon!'

She said: 'His melodies were always poured
out to him by the Winds from crystal cars,
his silence came from those dark Spirits who guard
the hidden ores,

from singing insects who nursed Sophocles
came solar honey when his mouth was open,
his chill came from the eyes of Arethuse,
flower of the Ocean.'

I said: 'In halls of Jove he seized the cloud,
Acroceraunian thunder and fire.
Do you not hear the rustle of our wood
offering a pyre?

The funeral preparations go ahead.
The pyre builds up without the axe's labour!
See boles and branches rushing up to crowd
upon the altar!

The fire that falls from heaven puts a light
to him. The resin splutters trickling down.
Its odour from the sea's edge reaches out
to the Alps' crown.'

She said: 'He comes to us, a castaway
sea-swept along from whirlpool to abyss,
for rest. See silent in the silent sky
what soul is his.

Calm yourself and your guest! That mortal singer,
who called up the great Niobe of stone
and heard the quarrel sliding from the quiver,
let that mere man

call up beside the silent castaway
the royal maiden who brought such distress,
Jocasta's daughter in the gentle play
of her white dress,

Antigone whose soul was made of light,
whose eyes were violet, the only one
whom he, when he had been cast grimly out,
still loved alone.

Here is the lily for that dead man's locks,
that flower so hard to conquer, that Tyrrhene
blossom bare Gombo bears, called by the Greeks
"the double game",

pancrazio.' Last I said: 'Leave it alone.
And let it lie untouched as on a grave,
watching over these Shades and their supreme
and holy love.'

# Terra, vale!

Now the whole Sky is sinking in the Sea.
Bright sea-banks turn themselves to shady caverns,
bedchambers for the Furies from Avernus.
Impenetrable clouds at ocean's limit
rise opposite to walls of swarthy basalt.
Between these two nights only Sea is shining.
Held very closely in the whirling eddies,
like a pale victim, there is still some light.

The tempest has uprooted in its fury
neptunian pasturage torn out of briny
valleys where backward monsters lie in wait.
Bluish algae, rust-coloured tangle, black
sea-lettuces with roots of many shapes
make huge obstruction at the stagnant mouth,
a floating meadow which no flock will browse,
and never to be trodden by a shepherd.

Perhaps some strength is hidden in the sterile
filaments to transform humanity?
Myth of the mortal made into a sky-
blue god, renew yourself once more in this
longing aroused in me by tireless waves!
Now the whole Sky is sinking in the Sea.
Light is the victim of the living eddies,
offered perhaps through all eternity.

# Second dithyramb

I was myself once Glauco from Anthèdon.
And in my inmost heart
I have felt godhead quiver, felt inside
my very bones the shiver
of oceanic vigour of a sudden
course through me, merest mortal
created out of substance that is fading,
offspring of dust and shadow!
My metamorphosis is always with me.
My mind, recalling it,
becomes a foaming ocean turning azure,
an ocean where the mouths
of all the thousand rivers flow together
over my head: the mighty
floodwaters as they meet once more dissolve
this complex bony structure.
Gods of the ocean depths, call back your exile
from where he lives so wretched,
his body moistened with such bitter blood,
on feet that weary stagger
and weakly linger over muddy pathways,
he who was once unconquered
strength of the ocean flood turned into rippling
muscles that turn and twist,
yes he to whom the currents of the Ocean
became a pastime, weaving
his own divine events and circumstances
over a glassy warp. O
Gods of the ocean depths, call back your exile
in all his gloom, and lave him
in lustral streams beneath and on the earth,
restore him in his godhead!

This I recall: evening was on the waters
already, but the farthest
skies flaming inextinguishable fire,
and all the gulfs and headlands
and islands opposite were growing blacker

like altars without victims
that instant as I paused upon the meadow
near to the ocean's edge.
Weighed down with my great catch, with no delay
I emptied out the knotted
threads on the grass to number my abundance.
Then from the heaped confusion
I laid out ordered lines. And I was happy
to see so many scales
shining through brown intricacy. 'My knotted
threads, my lead weights, my corks I
shall hang up in your temple, friendly god'
I said, I was so grateful.
And then I saw the fishes had more sparkle,
I saw the fins were twitching,
gills breathing in and out, and new strength coursing
over the scales and flashing.
And then, as when the power of Dionysus
flows into the Bacchantes
unleashing all their horde across the mountains,
the silent people seemed
uncannily stirred up into a rage,
into a sacred frenzy.
'What kind of miracle is this?' I shouted
aloud and in great terror;
for all my catch were vying with each other
to flee with viperine
rapidity, and leaping off away.
'Wretch that I am! Some god
is doing this? Or just the grass?' I waited,
astonished. And the silence
seemed to be godly in that solitude.
Evening was there already,
but stretches of the farthest skies were blazing.
I thought I heard the hollow
tritonian trumpet sound along the wooded
headlands; I seemed to listen
while fatal songs were spreading from the islands.
And then as if unconscious
I felt my hand run over those strange grasses,

the while within I pondered
the miracle. I tore the gloomy stalks
up by their roots; and avid,
as goats are for young shrubs and shoots, I started
to chew on them. And now the sap was streaming
into my throat, and streaming
into my heart, making a strange commotion.
I cried out, 'Earth!' And earth
smoked all about me as it were a cloud
upon the point of melting
from underneath my feet themselves so fleeting.
And then there rose a fearful
desire within me for the endless ocean,
for salt of bitter waters,
for gulfs, for whirlpools, and for windy eddies.
My flesh was shaken loose
from all terrestrial weight. From deep inside me
there came to birth the image
of waves without an end, and through my eyelids
I saw revealed the novel
splendour of azure blood, and neck and shoulders
appeared to be expanding,
knees to be joining up, and scales of fishes
growing to cover over
my skin, cold flashes running through my muscles.
'Terra, vale!' Headlong
I fell into the gulf, went under, touching
the lowest ocean valley,
a man no more, not yet a god, but mindless
of earth and earthly people.

Flowing rivers, I hear the heavenly murmur
you always make inside me,
flowing in many ways so very various –
softly in peace, or hoarsely
in violence, and hot perhaps as fresh
winds which have carried us
the copious deluge, or perhaps as chilly
as, fraught with snow, the summits
whence you have come untouchable, and tawny

with golden sands or reddish
with various clays, or fat with mud or clearer
than all the star-filled ether!
So in your hundreds you have travelled over
my head. All of the fluid
life of the globe has flowed across my prostrate
shoulders, with inexpressive
music. Even the Acheron, sad river
of Tartarus, was sweeping
along on its blind pallor stolen petals
from fields of asphodel.
All of the waters rumbled roared and gurgled
over and over, bearing
earthliness from this body quite forgetful
of its first tough existence.
I rose again, a god, up to the sacred
ether; I breathed one mighty
breath which impelled a ship of heroes, augur
and patron of the Argo!
Upon the prow, head bent, the Thracian singer
received the great prediction.
Near him, with flowing golden hair, and blooming
in youth and scarcely bearded,
(sensing his immortality his heart
bounded beneath his splendid
baldric) near Orpheus offspring of Apollo
was Pollux, Helen's brother.

Gods of the ocean depths, call back your exile,
restore him in his godhead!
I was myself once Glauco from Anthèdon.
The earth to me is anguish.
Look, all the light is in the Lower Sea,
and everywhere is shadow.
Herald of miracles, O ocean Daybreak!
I rush into the vortex.

# The oleander

## I

Erigone, Aretusa, Berenice,
now which of you accompanied the night
of summer with the most melodious music
in oleanders by the shining sea?
The ladies sat with us beside the sea
and each of them had her own kind of music
within her heart to match the friendly night;
and each of them seemed truly well at ease.

And we sat on the seashore, once emerged
from the clear waters with our blood revived
by their sharp salt; ambiguous oleanders
wove roses in among their regal laurel
upon our heads; the day with such great blessings
had so replenished us that we, content,
were smiling out our inexpressible
gratitude for the day as it lay dying.

'The Day' said Erigone very softly,
turning towards the light 'can never die.
His face appeared to us so very clear;
he never showed such gentleness before.'
Her simple way of speech was like the wind
of summer when it slakes our thirst in gulps,
and in its pauses we recall the fountains
of the far gardens whence it comes to us.

I heard her, but as I were still submerged
with her voice coming through a humid veil.
So I reclined my cheek and, warm as blood,
out of the twisted hollow of my ear
came the sea-water gushing all at once.
And, sinking down into the sand my naked
feet, I could feel departing very slowly
the gentle heat: the sun by now had set.

And who cut off a branch of oleander?
I did not turn round, but the rather bitter
lymphatic fragrance from the newly opened
wound reached my nostrils, and it overcame
the musky scent of the vermilion flowers.
'O Glauco' Berenice said 'I am thirsty.'
And Aretusa said: 'O Derbe, when
did roses bloom on the triumphal laurel?'

She knew when well enough, but Derbe did not,
inexpert in devising lucid fable.
And my heart in its depths began to shudder,
shudder and shake with godlike poetry.
So I began to pray: 'O all my longings,
ravenous race and wakeful, go to sleep!
Give your consent that I, during your slumber,
may crown myself with the triumphal laurel!'

Then everything swelled up, even my heart.
Oh poetry, you are a godlike freedom!
The Alps were rising, all their thousand summits,
with the momentum of as many eagles,
such bursting forth of such impetuous strength
from out their stubborn viscera of marble
whence he who did not wish for human offspring
extracted his imperishable children.

And the curved ramifications of the Alps
were stretching out as to embrace the sea;
and the sea sparkled in its fabulous
candour inside the crescent-moon-shaped gulf
with the same beauty that our ladies had.
And that light fashioned out of you a myth
reborn in the irradiated world,
Erigone, Aretusa, Berenice!

So that we seemed to hear once more the song
the Sirens sang, hear from our hollow ship –
the swift, the dark-blue-prowed, the strongly rowed –
in an unhappy voyage of return
pushed by the wind on breakers of the sea;

104

nor did Odysseus save us from the peril
with wax inside our ears; but this heart rather,
no longer free, was filled once more with longing.

## II

'O Glauco' Berenice said 'I am thirsty.
Where is the fountain? and where are the fruits?
Where is Cyane azure as the air?
Where will you pluck again with your own hands
the golden orange in its gloomy foliage?
O how we slaked our thirst! How many times
our thirst was slaked! And then we liked so much
the slaking of the thirst that we desired
more burnèd thirst. Who had a skill like ours?
distinguishing the flavour of each fruit
and its maturity just by the colour?
distinguishing the freshness of the waters
and picking out the coolest spring of all?
and shaping lips to cope with varied draughts
and modulating sips as they were notes?
I loved the image of myself in water.
I burned with self-love as I bent across,
I was so pretty in the nymphine glass.
I was Cyane azure as the air.
You seized me in among the swimming foliage.
The godly gloomy deeps transfigured me.
A sudden flower opened its petals out
between my knees. I was enchained and tangled
in green intricacies, in roots as pallid
as my own feet, in hidden inner chill.
The sungod shining through transfigured me.
Innumerable rings upon my fingers
were fashioned from his rays, combs in my hair,
necklaces at my throat, a dress of gold.
O Aretusa, why was I not you?
Were you born on the island of Ortygia
as the belovèd of the raging river?
The drink you brought refreshed the scaly Siren,
when evening had come down, when flutes were silent.

I grew the reeds the shepherds use for flutes.
I was Cyane azure as the air.
The spring of water stayed within my eyes;
the sluggish current slowly polished me.
O Glauco, you remember Sicily?'
And I could see no more the lofty Alps,
the shining sea. I said: 'Let us go there!'

'Do you recall the handsome Doric lady
in golden effigy named Syracuse?
with all her dolphins and with all her horses,
crown of the sea? We sighted one fine day,
standing on Achradina, the trireme
bringing to us from Ceos the new Ode
Bacchylides had made the victor king.
We heard borne on the wind the sound of the flute
which harmonized the movement of the oars,
we heard then did not hear the raucous song
the boatswain always sang; while silently
the Ode, made out of everlasting words,
and lighter than a garland of wild olive,
loaded the keel and weighted it with glory.
We went down to the port. The hour was late,
Ortygia's acropolis a blazing pyre;
clouds were on fire by Cape Plemmirio,
as fine as statues on the pediments
of the temples; the huge arc of the sea
seemed a bow stretched by the strength of Syracuse.
And we cried out, and suddenly a clamour
ran all along the colonnades: the ship
fraught with eternity had come to port.
She bore us glory, and she was alive,
magnanimous, sublime. Along her benches
the slavish panting carried on and on;
along the ranks in tiers there could be seen
the naked oarsmen smeared with olive oil:
out of the portholes breathed their mighty effort;
the oar where it was held in slanting rays
gleamed like the shoulderblade; a savage smell,
a smell of savage beasts, was spreading round.

106

And it was not from all that slavish panting
that the ship was alive, not from the blood
and all the heavy bones within its hull:
she was alive, a god, because of one
thing she was carrying from overseas
to Hieron, king, victorious charioteer;
she was alive, magnanimous, sublime,
because of one thing brought from overseas,
and lighter than a garland of wild olive:
the Ode, made out of everlasting words.'

'That is all true!' I shouted. 'I remember.'
And my heart in its depths began to shudder,
shudder and shake with godlike poetry.
'I recall. It was the Ode made for a triumph:
"Celebrate Demeter who rules the fertile
Sicilian plains, and celebrate her daughter
girdled with violets! Celebrate, Clio,
who know best how to give immortal fame,
the race that Hieron's horses ran and won!
Nike, Aglaia went with them: they travelled
fast as the wind..."' The soul with swollen canvas
of dreams was sailing for the distances
of time towards the glorious landing-places
fraught with eternity just like that ship
from Ceos. We passed the hellesponts, the gulfs,
the islands, archipelagos, the syrtes:
we reverenced the mouths of our paternal
rivers, we prayed the sacred promontories,
we greeted the white citadels that Pallas
Athene watches over on their rocks,
we travelled overland by the Diolkos.
We saw the heroes there and Pindar with them.
And we forgot the nightingale of Ceos,
all for the eagle out of Thebes. Your fabled
light shone upon the Tyrrhene Sea, O Mother
Hellas, the Alps of Luni were as splendid,
though naked, as your mountains were, O Mother
Hellas, as splendid as your ever-glorious
mountains, whence there came down to you the race

of the Immortals who walked by the side
of the Ephemerals across affliction
which was subdued, and these and those were equal,
and all were Hellenes and in one divine
language they were all speaking, men and gods.

We watched in silence with the famous myths
issuing cloud-like from the Alps of Luni
and moving down towards the shining sea.
Then I saw Pegasus: one moment he
planted his feet high up upon the marble,
and then he leapt into the blue, immense
wings spreading far and wide, without a rider;
and from his breast and belly, both enormous,
transpired a sort of palpitating flame,
the potency of his gorgonian blood.
Ardi cried out: 'Look, there is Orpheus' head,
the Hebrus-borne!' The seashore seemed to await
after his cry the accomplishment of fate.
It grew in beauty with that sacred fear.
The wave was unbelievable and clear,
in a refulgence never parallelled.
A day not doomed to die shone on the world.

### III

But heart could not endure – too weak and mortal
for that great silence – and it turned instead
towards the ladies then, who were all smiles.
And Derbe said to Aretusa: 'When
did roses bloom on the triumphal laurel?'
Now she in all her pride of youth was standing,
that changing wave of the sea with face of gold,
in oleanders; and the severed branch –
on her moist hair which streamed on all sides down
and simulated round her open face
the rolling ripples of an ancient fountain –
wove roses in among the regal laurel.
'I shall explain to you' said Aretusa,
that changing wave of the sea with face of gold.

She said: 'The god Apollo hunted Daphne,
as poets tell it, all along the river.
The daughter of the river-god was panting
and crying out for rescue to her father.
From time to time her rapid legs got tangled
in her long hair: she nearly tumbled over.
Just so the filly out of Thessaly
gallops: her tawny mane, streaming out free
and reaching to the ground, is cause of bother.

The rapid god Apollo presses hard,
his longing flaring up to prey on her.
And at the hot breath of the blazing god
the frightened girl feels flames invade her hair.
She cries: "O father, you be my safeguard!"
And as she cries her voice is lost in air.
"Father, I'm captured by a rapid fire!"
She runs, she pants, and her smooth legs inspire
more fury in the god to prey on her.

"Peneios, my great father, I am lost,
I'm growing weak about the knees. Oh free
me from this fire burning so very fast,
so fast that now, now look, it's grasping me!"
And yet her young blood thinks that it knows best:
young blood and beauty talk quite differently
Her heart leaps up, she buckles at the knees.
And now she stops and, closing up her eyes,
shudders and says: "I give myself for lost."

A kind of joy is added to her terror,
which lends her godlike peril much more speed.
Naked but for her hair, she hears the quiver
and arrows rattle on the running god,
she senses all the strength of her pursuer,
sees ardour through closed eyelids and, half-read-
y to be seized, no longer calls her father.
But "Daphne! Daphne! Daphne!" Apollo calls her.
A more attractive voice she has not heard.

The god calls: "Daphne, Daphne!" And she dares
to open up her eyes: vermilion-faced
the god is, seen close to, his wide mouth nears,
and then in his embraces she's enlaced.
Transported by the gleaming god perforce
she gives a shout resounding through the waste
for one last time: Peneios now responds.
Greedy for nakedness the god unwinds
the hair by which her body is embraced.

White pith or marrow within bark that gleams,
grapes that in dense vine-leaves are delicate!
The god subdues her bareness, but it seems
that quite unconsciously she's holding out.
Her tender breast yields to him; but it seems
that from the belly down she's taken root,
and she stands stiff unmoving in the soil.
Her lover, thunderstruck, lets his arms fall.
"O wretched Daphne, rooted to the spot!"

All of a sudden Daphne's taken fright:
her face and breast are turning green and pale.
She looks about to fall; but the one joint
her knees have stays hard and it stays quite still.
She flounders but in vain. The act of flight
wrenches her sides in vain. The very feel
of her own life has sunk into the ground.
Her disappointed lover wraps her round.
"O Daphne, who is changing you about?"

But not the god with his melodious wail
suffices to extract her from her fate.
And in the moisture of the savage soil
she feels her feet to tangled roots contort
themselves till from their juncture she can feel
a trunk arise which clutches to include
her legs up to the barky thighs, and there
where her virginity should be in flower
compose a knot will never be untied.

She groans "Apollo" in her latest grief
"take me! Has all your lust just disappeared?
O Phoebus, are you not the son of Jove?
Are you not, Silver Bow, yourself a god?
Capture me, snatch me from this dreadful earth
which takes me to itself and drinks my blood!
You have pursued me in your lust and fury
and now you do not want me, lost, unlucky!
Save me in honour of the lust you had!

Save me, Apollo, only out of pity!
Make, if you loved this hair that wrapped me round,
a bow-string from the hair of your loved lady!
Take me, Apollo!" And she reaches out
her leafy hands; the green spreads; and already
each arm up to the elbow is a bough;
the green and brown are covering her skin;
navel and breasts – her cries are all in vain –
have turned into a stubborn trunk by now.

"Help, help! My heart is held inside a vice.
Look what black bark is holding my chest in!
O Phoebus, snatch me from this earth at once!
Will not lust serve to clutch me once again?
I'm naked, take me now on this soft grass,
on this soft grass on this soft hair of mine.
I burn with love for you as you for me.
Apollo, god Apollo, why delay?
I feel I am all over turning green."

That soft hair is already fresh green frond
arranged about a face that's changing colour.
Peneios' daughter is no longer blonde;
no more a nymph, nor yet a laurel either.
Only her mouth that still laments is red
and fragrant with a strange and fresh aroma.
And words find out their way mingled with tears
scented with her last cry. O mouth, first rose
blooming upon the bay which blooms in summer!

Her body flows green lymph; there but remains
blood in the lips which call and cry spasmod-
ically. Pale fibres rather than dark veins
come from her heart: only her mouth is red.
Lust pricks her lover but he is restrained.
He sees she is his tree but seems afraid
to touch; he hears her but he has no power.
And then she does not call him any more.
The god calls "Daphne! Daphne!" without end.

There's no response: her voice is silenced; even
that once-melodious throat is turned to wood.
Her eyelids are two little trembling leaves;
her eyes are two drops of arboreal fluid;
and brownish ridges roughen up her cheeks;
her nose has left no trace in that rough wood.
But in the shade her mouth is blood-red still,
Daphne's mouth in the shade of laurel still
burns and is offered to the panting god.

He turns towards her burning; he is bowed;
he kisses her impetuous with desire.
The tree is trembling from its roots; the shade
around the godlike forehead turns to fire;
the boughs stretch out; the forehead of the god
is laurelled with the leaves those branches bear.
Io Paean! Glory! But he can feel
under his kisses only living green,
bitter berries. And calls her name once more.

"O wretched Daphne, rooted to the spot!
And made almost irrelevant to me!
Your flesh is changed, that was so sweet and soft,
to rugged trunk and gloomy greenery.
Your bright vermilion mouth is getting blurred,
that seemed a flame flaming eternally.
However light upon the grass they were,
your feet are rooted now in this black earth!
Do you hear, Daphne? Why not answer me?

Answer me! Answer me!" The leaves but shudder
up at the tree's top. Silence. And a brief
murmur is heard. "Daphne, why don't you answer?"
A lighter quiver moves the top of the tree.
Then all is still again, the banks of the river
under a wide sky silent as can be.
The glorious laurel is not murmuring;
but the god's anguish rises up in song.
Mountains and valleys hear the song in peace.

Mountains hear it and valleys and the woods
and fountains and the islands and the rivers.
The song from his enamoured being spreads
bringing to birth each living thing that prospers.
The beauty that was Daphne overspreads
this earth of ours; and Daphne's delicate members
are mountain valley wood river and fount,
her glance ensapphires the horizons round,
her hair makes gold to ripen in our summers.

Daphne, now both the god and singing man
will want no honour but a sprig of bay
from you! And so the Bow of Silver, when
his heart is calmed in the immensity
of hymning, soothed and sated, lies till dawn
dawns for him underneath this sacred tree.
Night falls. Over Apollo in his sleep
the tree is shining with a blood-red gleam,
as bronze, glowing red-hot, is used to shine.

Between Olympus and Ossa – the night flies –
see one star set, another star arise.
Mysteriously the tree blushes like fire
while heavy dews are falling on the blaze.
Apollo sleeps and dreams of his desire,
of Daphne, and his heart imagines joys.
And the day dawns. The god gets up: a roar
of wild surprise irradiates the shore.
The laurel flashes out with rose on rose!'

## IV

She told us of the laurel and its rose –
that Aretusa who was Florentine,
that changing wave of the sea with face of gold.

Her voice flowed for us like the argentine
water that waters lavender or mint
or sage or other herbs in early dawn.

Furrowed and fed by that pure rivulet
'The oleander is the crown for me'
I said. So Aretusa was content,

cutting another pair of boughs away,
making as if to fashion me a wreath:
'In honour of your latest poetry!

Praying that in your heart you'll always have
the blue and tawny Summer and your rhymes
like wildest of wild roses come to birth!'

It seemed that day of summer could not die:
it went on smiling on the shining sea,
silent and with no end at all in sight;

the summer night, treated unequally,
watched its opponent from the heights, as blue,
Cyane, as you ever thought to be.

Sadly enraptured, almost drunk, whom too
powerful fountains cast their spell upon,
we looked towards our ladies as men do.

But Melancholy came and settled down
with us among the oleanders, mute
and staring at us with a steady frown.

And Erigone, who already knew
that taciturn companion to all thought,
inclined her head like one who says hello.

And told us of the mystery and Night.


V


'The Day' she said 'can never ever die.
His blood has failed to stain the shining sea.
His face appeared to us so very clear;
he never showed such gentleness before.
He is lying back upon the shining sea,
smiling upon the sky which was his realm,
waiting some unknown death or joy, his charm
being such that Night, so gloomy and obscure,
so far from quenching is enflamed by him,
and holds him golden in her circling arm,
covers and hides him with her head of hair,
but only so his members all of gold
are clearly visible through that great gloom,
enlightening the peaceful sky of night.
The hot winds breathe upon the shining sea,
and the hot streams are streaming slowly on
into the dreadful cities, to their heart,
to pass away flowing through unknown plains,
round unknown woods: the stags are coming down
to drink and pant in the oppressive heat;
they hear protracted belling in the distance;
they drink: at last in some secluded glade
there will be bitter fighting to the death.
O Night, O Night, it is in vain you take
your enemy into hiding in your hair!
Your hair's not so luxuriant and thick
that human eyes like ours cannot perceive
your pleasure flaming through it everywhere.
The earth, drunken with night, can hardly breathe.
The shade is burning. Vines are just like wine:
the cluster on the tendrils is maturing

115

because the ray is prisoned in the grapes.
The earth is cumbered with its drunkenness.
The shade is burning like a glaucous flame.
Life and death meet upon the shining sea,
enormous cradle and enormous tomb;
the source runs from the mountain down to him.
Under the tears of night the Pleiades
are growing pale and one of them concealed,
the one whose happiness has brought her shame.
Orion is unbuckling his armour,
Boötes turns, the very Cynosure
is flickering; and the Bear itself grows dim.
Night is oblivious of all her stars
and of the ancient pain of human lovers.
That we shall weep with her she does not know.
O Night, you should lament all of your stars!
The cry made by the skylark in the morning
will certainly disjoin us from our love.'

There was another with us, who stayed mute,
in oleanders by the shining sea.

# Mouth of the Serchio

### ARDI

Glauco, Glauco, where are you? I can't see
you any more. The path is lost. My horse
is stopping. Pines and pines in all directions
constrict me. Agrio sinks in the mass
of needles, as he'd sink in sand, up to
the fetlocks. But where are you, Glauco? Can
you see me? Both my legs bleed. We were mad
to enter naked in the wood, as though
it were the sea. The brambles, brushwood, scales
tear at us, and rough junipers. Don't you
bleed also? What a scent! It rises sudden-
ly like a flame. It is the wine of Summer!
I've drunk one full cup, and I'm drinking now
another, now a warmer one, and now
one boiling so it burns my heart and fills
me to the throat, up to the very eyes.
O Glauco, drink the heady wine of Summer
mixed with the gold of resin and of honey!

### GLAUCO

Yes, Ardi, I can see you. You look handsome
upon your white horse. And although you cannot
in these days wear the chlamys, like those horsemen
of Athens, yet it suits you to be naked.
Force Agrio on! There is no path. The boles
break just as easily as dried-up reeds.
Can't you hear Folo break them with his breast?
But then perhaps you fear the scales and brambles
on the marble of your legs? Your blood looks splendid,
Ardi. Since everything around expresses
its richest and most secret properties
for your intoxication, let it not
grieve you to bleed as the pine oozes resin,
as the juniper spreads its scent. Push on, push on
where all the woodland reddens and gives way!
Did you ever see more tawny hair, more thick?

117

Pleasant dreams are belated there like bees
caught in the tangles of a lion's mane.


ARDI

It is my hair that's caught. Oh look, the bough
is breaking, needles rain upon my neck,
and on my shoulders; they already cover
Agrio's back. You see? Thousands of them!
All of the bifurcated boughs are laden,
in every joint dead needles building up
into great heaps. To me all of this woodland
seems to be dead, and quite dried up, and blind.
Like glass it shatters. And the green is up
above, invisible, where the sun's rays
are put in prison; but its shadow bakes
my forehead and it dries my nostrils up.
We shall go in the river with our horses!
And splash about in the middle of the stream!
Is the Serchio far off still? All the shade
breathes out aridity. No water's near.
And I sense that the hoof which travels over
dead needles will find nothing much beyond
but burning sand. The empty cones are black
as bits of burnt-out coal, as long-extinguished
embers. Where, Glauco, are you leading me?


GLAUCO

Now close your eyes. D'you hear the wind? You feel
as if you travel under sail a desert
sea. Can you hear wind in the shrouds? And hear
the groaning of the masts under the stress
of crowded canvas, sailing treacherous
waters which take us to the isle of Circe?
In our clay pitchers not a drop remains
of water from the spring. We shall drink salt.
Open your eyes! Here is the atrium
of the enchantress glittering with marvels.
Phantoms of stars adorn the regal palace
of Circe, solar lady, see them?, like
leaves that have rotted in the autumn rains

118

and still preserve their delicate nervation
with all the thinness of fine linen woven
from air and light. Thin palpitating threads
are joining them; the rainbow alters them;
inexpressible trembling twitches them.
Circe has charmed the highest stars, and held them,
and emptied out their incandescent substance;
and here she brings their tenuous ghosts together.


ARDI

The work of spiders, artistry of gods,
star-paintings! Glauco, I've already torn
one with my face, and now another. Look!
There are stars woven for us everywhere.
We're taken in innumerable nets.
Stop here! And let us not destroy the charm.


GLAUCO

The glade is near at hand. The sun gets through
between the boughs. Everything shakes and sparkles.
The resin on the trunk is just like amber.
The closed-up myrtle shines like polished metal.
The tamarisk seems almost to be azure
among the red pines. And your face is pearled.


ARDI

And oh how handsome Folo is who crosses,
speckled with sweat, out of the shade and into
the band of sunlight! You are bleeding too.
Didn't you see the vipers moving off?
What is the name of these long stalks of grass
each with a sable ear upon the top?


GLAUCO

The name is one which will delight your lips.
Release the reins and let them lie upon
Agrio's neck. And listen: in the silence
the horse is snorting. Its slaver flies and whitens
the wild mint. Why should this, I wonder, Ardi,
suffice to fill my breast with happiness?

### ARDI

We were perhaps once children of the Cloud.
The grass was trampled once beneath our hooves;
we picked the flower with fingers that were human.
One day, turning our naked torsos round,
with a curved piece of bark we washed away
from off the hide of overheated rumps
the sweat which trickled down in rivulets.
Enormous space was our intoxication.
With ease our indefatigable flanks
went faster than the trembling of the wind.
As much of earth we covered in one day
as Pegasus could cover of the sky.

### GLAUCO

Rapidity, Rapidity, most joyful
triumph over the grievous burden, airy
fever, thirst for the wind and all its splendour,
spirit accumulated in a mass
of bones! Rapidity, first to be born
from the strung bow which people know as Life!
Ardi, our lives should go by at a gallop:
cross over all the rivers, find them out
from source to mouth, and then along the shores
of ocean print our hooves upon the winding
token, the silver line, the only trace
the latest wave has left there of itself.

### ARDI

Were we permitted happily to cover
the Universe! Our breast is too constricted,
however, by the panting of the soul.
O Glauco, to the one who hears you, you
are like the unrelenting fly which goads
the herd. And the horizon is a ring
of glass you shatter in your great disdain.

### GLAUCO

Let us not talk, but drink the wine of Summer,
given up solely to the river's love.

I sigh for all the woodlands of the Earth;
but if in one as a recluse I had
to live, Ardi, in this one I would choose
to live, in this hot wood which faces south,
in this aridity of burning shade.

ARDI

It is a pyre about to burst in flame.
The power of fire is closed in it and smoulders.
It murmurs very gently in the breeze,
but its true voice is silently withheld.
It will speak out with tongues of conflagration
when clouds engendered in the Tyrrhene Sea
scatter their lightnings on it in the night.

GLAUCO

The breath does not pass through the gullet only,
but goes through every limb, down to the toes
of the bare foot; and all the scents transpire
through every pore. I sense my horse's breathing,
and sense at times its savage animal
happiness, just as though inside the double
body one heart alone, my heart, were burning.

ARDI

Here is the grass, the greenness, and a reed.
Here is a grassy track. There, in the background,
look at the Pisan Hills looking so angry,
all clouded over under showers of rain.

GLAUCO

Cannot you hear the croaking of the crows
there near the sea? They go towards the Serchio's
mouth in great numbers, where the nets are spread,
as I am told by the huntsman of Vecchiano.

ARDI

The Serchio then is near? Follow the signs.
Here is the sand, with scattered junipers,
untouched by footprints as it were a desert.

Is the mouth hidden in the beds of reeds?
And will we come upon it all at once?
Will it delight us? No, we need not hurry!
Slow to a walk. For the desire is pleasant,
and comes to us from long forgetfulness,
comes from the ancient sanctity of water.
We are at liberty in the forest, naked
on swift obedient horses, full of hope
the god may show to us unchanging splendour.
No, do not hurry, for the heart is full.

GLAUCO

O famous mouths of venerable floods!
Along by Ostia's fallen stones the Tiber
is more divine. The Arno in my music
flows smoothly. And my own Aterno, purpled
with sails, gleams splendidly like hostile blood.
I've seen Eridanus, Achelous,
and the great Delta, and mouths which have no name
where dreams the pilgrim dreamed were more than anxious
to stay. But may the god permit this one
to be the very finest of them all;
for never was my breast harmonious,
never before so worthy to reflect
unchanging splendour as the god reveals it.

ARDI

A mystery! The green precincts receive
your vows, the antechamber to a silvan
temple. The pines lift up their shady columns
around the sacred liminary lake
which has an emerald meadow for its bed.
Down into it and into silence sinks
the image of the sky: it does not laugh
or smile, but from the depths looks up intently.

GLAUCO

D'you hear the tune of the Tyrrhenian Sea?
Among the voices of most distant seas,
in my extreme old age, in the near horror

of the last frost, my blood will copy it.
And this cerulean tawny Summer I
shall always have at heart. Hear the low song
providing company along this narrow
isthmus formed like the yoke across a lyre.

ARDI

The whole is godlike music, a responsive
instrument to the endless breath. Now look
at broken reeds across the sand, and look
at torn-up roots, still trembling from the touch,
the breath, of puckered lips and skilful fingers!
Ephemeral musicians in the reeds
have just now ceased to play the fluvial song.

GLAUCO

Ardi, dismount. Here is at last the river,
yes here the mountain-born. It is a marvel!
It carries in its mouth assembled sand,
and it is coloured like a laurel leaf.
We offer these young horses now to you,
O Serchio, and we offer too our bodies
containing as they do the heat of noon.

ARDI

We panted, such our strong desire to reach you!
It seemed at times, O river, that you must
gush from us like an unexpected hymn.

GLAUCO

You are a god, a god; and we are mortal.
But we shall cleave your current in our course.
True joy is always on the other bank.

# The stag

Do you not hear the dark interrupted belling
beyond the Serchio? Where the black-hoofed stag
is separating from its herd of females
and taking refuge in the wood. Soon he
will sleep on a green bed, deep in the thicket,
drawing through wrinkled nostrils his aggressive
breath with its wild aroma of wild mint.
And do you know the footprints he has left
are shaped most like a beating crimson heart?
He gives the impressionable earth that stamp;
and the imprinted turf, which he lifts up
with every hoof, he then lets fall again.
With reason this is called 'the great mark' by
the cautious huntsman who can read therein
the signs; his judgement never ever fails him,
and he is happy that he can pursue
this noble chief until the stars have set,
and kill him while the sun is being born,
and see the enormous body palpitating
under the fangs of dogs, the branching horns
high on his forehead fighting their last fight!

But all in vain the sound of that dark belling
for us who sit among the fluvial reeds.
You will not fling yourself into the Serchio,
Derbe, to follow up the track; the cold
river will not be ploughed up by the double
furrow of arm and predatory laugh,
your muscles flashing proudly in the chill.
We are unarmed and satisfied with splendour,
bending to look into our hearts where roars,
more distant than the belling of the stag,
the age-old longing that we feel for spoil.
He leaves the herd and goes into the wood.
Fruit of famed loins perhaps, with branching antlers.
No longer does he vex with nascent horn
the bark. His crown is hard enough already;
his throat is darkening where a beard is coming

124

and shortly will be swollen with so much
belling. We'll hear upon the night his lengthy
bellowing like the bellowing of a bull;
and we shall hear the clamour of his lust
arising in the silence of the Moon.

# The hippocampus

Like a willow wand,
you supple Muse
withdrawn from the Choir
so furtively,
changeable Arethuse,
changeable wave of the sea,
with the golden face,
who leave the laurel in peace
for the oleander crown,
now feed your glittering salt
to Folo my horse whose eyes
are yellow amber,
Folo my horse whose sides
are greyhound-lean:
a wingless colt,
but fine as blood of Medusa!
Offer him salt
to creak as he crunches it,
O Aretusa;
hold your hand out bare
and open and without fear,
for he will take your offer
with lips more light
than his legs,
and they go like the wind.
He is scarcely licking,
as if he were drinking!
He is soaking
you in his pleasure; and your palm
scarcely senses, behind
his lips, the clean
teeth of the colt,
which can so gently
graze on the grass when it's calm
and gnaw the difficult
iron I use to restrain
his speed like the speed of a flame
across these waste
shores without rest.

As, to your taste –
nymph who thieve
from orchards – a hive
fragrant with honey
is never worth any-
thing like one unripe plum,
so the finest fodder to him
is less than a handful
of biting salt.
He is greedy for it rather,
Aretusa,
like a blunt-nosed goat.
Memories of the sea
may run in the blood of Folo.
Perhaps he is of the race
of the Hippocampi,
with scaly tail.
Though now all lightning and flame,
he used to be
silver let's say
or sky-blue or green
as the waves and strong
as the biggest of all.
And in the evening late,
at the rise of the planet
which grows,
at the rising of the breeze,
when, dripping with salt,
he had come up on the shore
in peace,
flailing his fishy tail
upon the sand
but with gentleness,
looking up shy as a lover,
and dribbling slaver,
he would softly eat,
with his neck inclined,
his seaweed out of the hollow
of the Siren's hand.

## The wave

In the tranquil bay,
woven with scales
that overlap close-packed
like the ancient armour
of the cataphract,
see the Sea
scintillate.
It seems to discolour.
To silver? to dark?
At a stroke,
with a blow fit to burst
the metal links, the blast
of the wind breaks it up.
That does not last.
The wave is feebly born,
and straight dies down.
The wind gets up.
Another wave is born
to disappear,
a lamb which browses
across the green:
a flake of foam
which leaps in the air!
But the wind comes back
to rise and redound.
Another wave
is born,
more smooth in its curve
than a maiden's womb!
See it throb, and climb,
and swell, and curve,
and glitter, and be inclined.
Its back is broad
with a crystal gleam;
its delicate crown
is ruffled,
the snowy mane
of a dark horse.

128

The wave the wind unleashes
falls apart,
rushing into the hollow
of the sounding furrow;
it foams, it whitens,
like scented flowers, it brightens,
it sweeps a floating meadow
of alga and sea-lettuce;
it stretches itself,
it rolls and tumbles, gallops;
it stumbles
into a wave the wind
has shaped of a different kind;
it obstructs it,
attacks it, surmounts it,
mixes with it, and grows.
With spray, with flakes of foam,
with splashes of colour,
the undertow boils;
it catches the eyes
with chrysoprase
and virid beryl
in enormous piles.
And it gives voice!
it rinses the ear, splashes,
it swashes, smacks, it crashes,
it roars, it laughs, it sings,
tunes, untunes,
welcomes and fuses
the sharpest discords
that sleep in the deep
of its spirals,
fine and free,
numerous, waving raving,
strong and malleable,
a creature that is alive
to enjoy
its fleeting
mystery.
Heard all along the shore

by its barefoot sister,
the light of step,
the smooth of leg,
rapacious Aretusa
who plunders fruit
and has her lap brimful of it.
Her heart of a sudden leaps
her gold face lights
up. She lets
go of the edge of her dress,
she bends
to the resonant call;
in the melody she forgets
her savage spoil,
her sour treasure,
and lets it fall.
She also enjoys
herself with the wave,
happy to thieve
on the dry land,
as all of the tang
of the seas were surging in her!

So, Muse, I sang the praise
of my Extended Stanza.

# The coronal of Glauco

## Mèlitta

There shines, where spotted leopards stand and wait,
a white and solitary craggy stone
where silent honey always trickles down,
a sort of sticky fountain running late.

My bathing-pool is there, well set apart;
my naked body finds its flavour in
gardens and orchards, while the marble-stone
old gods were made from is what colours it.

From top to toe I am that kind of tawny
white which can even fool a worker-bee,
with eyes the semblance of the Lydian sand.

Through all such varied gold my very tiny
soul opens like a flower quite naturally.
Men call me Mèlitta: I'm honey-blonde.


## Sour grapes

I do not feed upon the dripping comb.
I leave the wax and honey for the bee.
And yet I pick sour plums from off the tree,
and I am pleased with aromatic gum.

I like the tart milk too that's taken from
the early fig which only June will see
blacken. I'll give you two fresh lips for three
or four green beans: with them my heart will come!

Come up, climb on the boughs. Here, take my hand.
I'm scented like the citron bergamot,
most fragrant when I'm squeezed about the waist.

131

You're panting! I'm too high? I understand:
you're like that greedy fox we've heard about
who came to say: You're too tart for my taste.


*Nico*


To me your two white feet are charming toys
in fine warm sand where you delight to squat,
bringing to mind (they are so small and white)
the polished bones thrown fervently by boys.

– Alas, poor Nico's peeling in the blaze!
Your 'fine warm sand' has scorched my 'two white feet'.
And you think that a thing to laugh about!
But I shall catch you soon, for all your ploys.

– You are an ingrate. With what art the flames
have made the veins stand out upon your skin
and reddened your big toe and heel together!

– Watch out. Not numbered bones for fun and games
have I in store for you, rebellious one,
but, slave, a whip of Paphlagonian leather.


*Nicarete*


Glauco of Serchio, hear me now. Now all
these rods and lines and hooks all clean and bright
which never caught a barb or mackerel yet
I, Nicarete, hang on your white wall.

I also hang my unreliable
lead weights and corks up there for you, the net
which never caught a mull or turbot yet:
just tangle and seaweed were usual.


132

Glauco, the sea is stingy. My one wish is
to walk with you. In shade of curls my mouth
is strong and sinuous, it seems to me.

I'd like to walk between the bending rushes
with you, and with you pick to make a wreath
hibiscus near Lake Massaciùccoli.


### To Nicarete

Look, Nicarete, from Quiesa right
up to Montràmito the hilltops are
like bending rushes bending with the air,
like them made out of gold that has no weight.

Their very softness, hung between the bright
transparent water and a sky as clear,
is something rather felt than seen and, more,
a joy more strong for hiding from the light.

Lighting the silence up, the lunar disk is
ascending. Look, it is completely round,
while in the Lake the water-lily closes.

At first it's coloured pink like the hibiscus
blossom with which your loving head is bound:
later it imitates your naked shoulders.


### Gorgo

A guest who's not ungrateful, I am Gorgo,
bringing with me the scented Cyclades,
and bringing grapes and spices too in these
fine light and airy linens from Amorgo.

Glauco, I bring some wine of Chios for you,
such as you drank that day on the high seas

when, hung in clay, it very nearly froze,
swung on the sheets by west or south wind for you.

I bring a crown of ivy and white poplar
because I liked so much that ode of yours
where Procne on her island mourns the rape.

Now, naked in retsina's pleasant odour,
I want to dance for you, along these shores,
that fluvial ode to music of the pipe.


### To Gorgo

Gorgo, most naked in sequacious lawn!
Your dress complies with you, holds nothing back.
From navel to smooth pubis now you look
as if you were a wave just being born.

There is no shadow on your limbs at all:
from groin to armpit white without a mark.
You're polished like a pebble from the brook,
and like that ode of mine – symmetrical.

Dance me that supple dance out of Ionia
now while the Apuan Alps are turning red
and the Tyrrhenian sighs and colours up.

Hellas is here – Luni to Populonia!
It is as though I watched you while you poured
me wine of Greece in an Etruscan cup.


### The flautist

I found the flayed skin of that indiscreet
Phrygian called Marsyas hanging on a pine,
on reddened earth the knife of the divine
avenger and, nearby, the double flute.

134

Glauco, I took it up with beating heart.
And, all oblivious of the dreadful doom,
I dare within my garden now and then
even beneath the laurel blow this flute.

I often turn and look about me for
the god who might be quickly manifest.
And yet this lip is never known to tremble.

My hairs are standing up in sacred awe,
and still I feel through my tormented breast
the breath of Marsyas – the far from humble.


*Baccha*

Who's calling me? Who's seizing me? A thyrsus
is what I am, with leaves instead of hair,
shaken about by some outlandish power.
Rumpled, I kick my shoes off, and my dress.

Up to the clouds or down to the abyss!
Whether you're god or monster, I am here.
Centaur, for you I am a pale grey mare:
fill me with foal, who foam and neigh like this.

Triton, for you I am a sea-blue wife:
my tongue is salt like alga, and upon
where would be legs are sounding scales which squeeze me.

What's calling me? The wreathèd horn of night?
neighing from Thessaly? thundering Pan?
Naked, I burn, I freeze. Oh who will seize me?

135

## Stabat nvda Aestas

The first thing was I glimpsed her naked foot
gliding across burnt needles of the pine:
the air was scorched and in such agitation
as though it were a white flame pouring out.
Even cicadas held their peace. The brooks
became more hoarse. Resin, more copious,
like lamentation pouring down the boles.
I recognised the grass snake by its scent.

In the grove of olives I caught up with her.
I caught the sky-blue shadow of the boughs
on sinuous arching spine, the tawny hair
through the Palladian silver fly across
without a sound. On farther, in the stubble,
the skylark, bounding from the shaven furrow,
called out to her, called out her name throughout
the sky. So then I also called her name.

I saw her turn round in the oleanders.
She went into the reeds, a brazen harvest
closing itself behind her raucously.
On farther, by the sea, she caught and tangled
her foot up in the heaps of ocean straw.
She fell stretched out between the sand and water.
The western breeze blew foam up from her hair.
Huge she appeared in all her nakedness.

# Third Dithyramb

To you, great Summer, great delight of the alps and sea,
between such candid marbles and waters so easy and free,
naked, your airy limbs imbued with golden blood
scented with resin and laurel and ocean weed,
praise be!
O great pleasure in the sky in the earth in the sea
and in the flanks of the faun, O Summer, and in this poetry!
Praise be
to you who have heaped with your richest gifts our day
and over the oleanders stretch the sunset out
showing a prodigy!

You scorched with your foot the silent ocean grass,
you dried with your breath the rains that so swiftly pass,
between such candid marbles and waters so easy and free
you stood erect; you were huge, and even the tiniest lives
enjoyed your joy and everything seen through your wide eyes:
the leaves of the woods and the boles of the ships,
the resin flowing, and in the pines the growing
of the enclosed pine-seeds and the scales which were sealing them
tending to tawny, and the tracks of the birds in the loam
of the rivers, the shadows of flights over salty sands,
sands ridged like the curving palates of certain beasts,
sands pleasant to wind and wave like groin and pubis
lovingly,
sands imitating the work of bees
and arranged like honeycombs
in honeyless hives,
and the cuttlefish bone among brown carobs
whitening on the beach, among the dead medusae
the polished fishbone gleaming, the seashell
iridescent among corks and osiers,
pale with longing the clouds
languish from peak to peak
rock after rugged rock
like a voluptuous lady going to bed with slaves,
and the cable run through the red
hawsehole, the trawl net

rise alive and pulsating with fins, the rod
bend with the living weight, the great
strength of the muscles swell on shaggy arms,
a rough hand
see to the sheet,
the side of the ship bend like a swimmer's cheek
to the sail and its strong rebuke,
the wake change colour,
all the Tyrrhenian Sea in flower
flickering like high pastures at the breath of the wind from the west

O Summer, blazing Summer,
we loved you enough to be
happy like you in the sky in the earth in the sea,
with you to burn with joy on the face of the earth,
Summer that no one can tame,
deep of breath,
dearest daughter of Pan, love of the Titan the Sun,
harmonious,
melodious,
who tune the curving sounding gulf
as the player upon the lyre
tunes his instrument,
Demeter's lament
complaining of you
every summer solstice
for Proserpina, lost spring days!
O tawny beast,
O lioness flaming in the Skies,
huge savage Summer,
libidinous,
vertiginous,
you who fire the loins,
who aggravate the thirst,
who excite the passions,
Muse, Gorgon,
you who undo belts,
who gird garments up,
who unleash the dances,
Grace, Bacchante,

138

you who express the scents,
you who strengthen the poisons,
you who sharpen the thorns,
Hesperis, Erinys,
diverse deity,
the plaything endlessly
of the winds of the waves of the sand,
splendid when you are angry without a sound,
sharp to the taste in your torpor,
O all splendid and sharp to the taste under a thousand names,
made for me of the dreams Pan draws from the feverish world
when he raves on his sacred reeds
(the raving of human dreams),
divine in the spume of the sea and of horses,
in the sweat of pleasures,
in the perfumed weeping of the thirsty pines,
O Summer, Summer, I shall call you divine,
and with a thousand names I shall name you,
with a thousand praises
I shall praise if you hear my prayer,
if you permit a mere mortal to tame you,
permit me to see you in the flesh,
permit me a mortal to relish you on the enormous bed of the beach
between the alps and the sea,
naked, your ardent limbs imbued with golden blood
scented with resin and laurel and ocean weed!

# Versilia

Don't be afraid, man with the blue-
green eyes! I'm just Versilia bursting
free from her wood-nymph's bark, and thirsting.
Ready to let you touch me too!

You strip the peach and find it sweet
and revel in its naked flesh.
Through scales and knotty wood the fresh
scent of that fruit which melts the heart

came to my nostrils, came where my
tongue like a tender dripping leaf
against in all their strength my teeth
felt itself languishing away.

Did you dream of such sensitive
nostrils ever in such rough wood?
No you did not, but you enjoyed
cool shade, that succulent fruit you have,

and shadows which pine-needles make,
moving this way and that to please
the winds, and gentle on the eyes
as flying shadows on a lake.

I studied from behind my bark
you who I knew were not perceiving,
poor man, the beating of my living
lashes against your sunburnt neck.

At times a scale of the bark of the pine
is rather like a rough eyelid
opening suddenly in the shade
to allow a glance that is divine.

I am divine; and you, maybe,
I like. Unlike the hairy dread
Satyr upon the myrtle bed
or faun who chases after me.

140

But you maybe I like. Your skin
the blazing Sun has darkened gives
off a salt sea-water scent. Your legs
are smooth as polished bronze and slim.

Offer to me your basket made
of plaited rushes and high-piled
with peaches! I don't want them peeled,
so put away that crooked blade.

I know the way to bite the fruit
so's not to lose one drop of juice.
Then, lips still wet, I introduce
honey into man's famished heart.

Now put that biting iron away:
it spoils the taste. You do not prize
the fruits you have. The peaches, cherries,
the pears, the figs of Tuscany

are sweetly fraught, the apples too,
the apricots, the medlars, when
you strip them in the early dawn
veiled in the cold nocturnal dew.

I have not relished for some time
such plenty. Oh, gifts meant for me
are scarce. While you per contra see
boughs bending with the Claudia plum!

And I have nothing but the dull
pine-cone which keeps its seed sealed in.
It is so hard even a stone
does not help me to break the scale.

Man with the sea-blue sky-blue eyes!
Please let me fill myself right up
with those ripe peaches which you keep
in that rush-woven basket of yours.

141

I beg you! Pine-cones are no good
except for flinging at the jay
who's always chattering away
hoarsely. The rosin is not food.

But if you chew it at your leisure,
although it has a bitter taste,
then when your dreaming heart's at rest
and free from every earthly pressure,

you will enjoy it most; and that
rosin I'll give you is most rich.
Meanwhile perhaps you'll give the peach,
whose juice is oozing out of it,

which I've not tasted for an age,
to me: I'm dying with the wish.
Don't be afraid. I am all flesh,
though cool and fresh as foliage.

Touch me. Your hands are quite without
fur and curved claws, oh quite unlike
some I have known. And my hair, look,
plum-like is flecked with violet.

My teeth are regular, more white
than pine-nuts newly shelled. And you
need have no fear, man with the blue-
green eyes! Just so you hold me tight,

as the horny shaggy Satyr does.
Under these branches we can hide,
and may these myrtles be our bed,
with white vitalba over us.

Why are you always on the alert?
Are you devoted to Diana?
Now coming down Pietrapana
is rapid September with his flute,

and the cornelian cherry's full
of blood-red berries, pungent fruit.
Behind the magpie's raucous shout
I think I hear the roebuck call.

Are you a hunter? Is the blow-pipe
your weapon, or the crossbow rather?
See, coming down Pietrapana,
September. Give your basket up.

I've seen bay hides through bush and brake
making towards the Serchio!
You give your basket up. I know
the spoor although I cannot bark.

Fit arrow to the string and pull.
If I love you, you shall have prey!
One grass-blade at my lips and I
can copy any creature's call.

# The death of the stag

Evening had almost come. I had been waiting
in ambush for the stag too long, crouched hidden
among the tedious reeds. All of a sudden
I saw the man crossing the Serchio, swimming.

A man it was for sure, and yet I felt
flesh prickle as the scent were bestial.
His hairy head and beard were of a pale
millet-like red; his shaggy armpits smelt;

but different skin from that upon the cheek
began below the belly, beastly fur
apparently; his nether regions were
enormous too, it seemed, thighs legs and feet;

he seemed to be some monster in a dream,
so great was the displacement of the swimmer
although he held both arms out of the water
and all his trunk erect above the spume.

He was a man. Some ducklings in a fright
made me quite sure, because they made him laugh.
Then suddenly he leapt that almost-cliff,
the river-bank, and landed on four feet!

I recognized him, trembling like a leaf.
The lusty generation of the Cloud:
twofold; above the waist a man indeed;
a stallion with huge scrotum all beneath.

The Centaur! Mantle mainly millet-like
in colour, tail and crupper roan, white flecks
on the extremities of but two legs,
with human back and horse back in an arc.

He had a rounded headpiece, which was thick
with curls like lustrous clusters of the vine,
and bent it to one side to gnaw upon
tall crests and crop the tender tendrils back

144

with wide mouth far more used to bloody victuals,
to grinding at huge bones, to drinking down
at one draught gallons of the smoky wine –
whole mixing bowls from Thessalian tables.

His human arm was raised, with biceps flashing,
to choose a twig from off a poplar-bough.
Sudden he started at a gallop through
the trees and disappeared among them, swishing.

I shook in every limb, my heart was pounding
my chest. And in my damp green hiding-place
ancient urges were making my thoughts race.
And then I heard the belling stag resounding!

I heard him belling in his pain and anger
as if a lion's fangs had torn his side
wide open. And I bounded from my bed
of reeds, at one bound conquering my horror,

through the red undergrowth, as smooth and fleet
as greyhound, through the brakes of juniper,
with silent speed, almost as though I were
dreaming, with pads of felt upon my feet.

O Derbe, metals fire has mastery over
have all the potency that I desire.
Shall I present to you the things I saw
made in Corinthian bronze to last for ever?

The Centaur in the brawl had seized upon
the enormous branching antlers of the stag,
as a man grasps his enemy's hair to drag
him from behind until he treads him down

to earth and manages to break his back
and kick his skull in underneath his heel,
or as a stallion in a sexual
frenzy bestrides a mare in his attack.

145

His hands in hair and horn of the stag's head,
rearing his trunk above it, and the stag's
body held pincered by just two horse-legs,
he held it down to earth with his great load.

The angry stag struggled to free himself
from under, eyes turned back, his swarthy neck
swollen with bellowing rage, with each rough shake
he gave shaking the flaky foam to earth.

One of those beasts sweet-sounding pipes would tame,
descendant of a very ancient race,
with body mighty as a buffalo's,
with twenty points on each egregious beam.

Oh moons of autumn, many a rival he
had hunted out from his delightful lair,
and pinned him to an oaktree's bark, before
he found that twofold creature in his way!

He shook and shook, and managed to break loose.
His bellowing resounded all around.
Leaving some antler in the monster's hand,
he ran a while; and then he turned his face.

He turned to make a fight of it, and heat
breathed from his nostrils with the hope of blood.
The Centaur, throwing down the splinter, stood
cautious and resolute on all four feet.

A thread of scarlet trickled slowly down
his human breast, and down the horse's hair
his sweat. And shining out, now less now more,
his crupper gleamed like copper in a sun

shedding its rays obliquely, striking hard,
now here now there according to the leaves.
Silence had fallen on the deepest groves.
Only the steady panting was still heard.

146

The needles of the pines seemed to be glowing
like dying embers on the battlefield.
And the sour bestial stench upon the wind
was mingled with the scent of resin flowing.

All of his strength held steady on the ground,
the stag, as though he were an angry bull,
lowered his antlered head. The Centaur's tail
struck three times whip-like at the air around.

A tawny ramified rapidity
hurled itself forward with a death-like bell.
O Derbe, my anxiety is still
for all the hazard of humanity!

I truly thought I heard a human groan
above the rearing up of that wild horse.
But then the Centaur with inhuman force
had tamed the stag's wild energy again.

Had seized him by his forehead, there where his
antlers took root, and wrenched the muzzle round.
Both of them towering up, the one combined
with the other in a tangle, the two foes –

in light and shade, under a sky all mute
and shot across and streaked with crimson splashes –
death-struggled; and above the swaying masses,
above the hooves the antlers the thick coat

the hairy mane the overbearing yard,
I saw the rising head of humankind,
and how his ringlets, all dishevelled, fanned
that wind of anger on to my own head.

Fraternal heart swollen with old remorse,
from my ambush I bent the bow to shoot.
But the man with his bare hands had forced apart
and torn up from the roots his enemy's horns.

147

I heard the strident tearing of the bone
being broken, broken open to the jaw.
Out of the skull, mingled with crimson gore,
the smoking brains themselves came gushing down.

The body tumbled with a hollow thud
and lay at rest; it bled without a sound;
it lay without a throb; it bathed the ground,
so parched and piny, with the burning flood.

He laughed as he had laughed upon that gaggle
light swimming on the verdant Serchio's stream.
Then raised, enormous in the sylvan gloom,
the double trophy gathered in his struggle.

He snuffed the wind. A little while he stayed
to pluck three branches loaded with their cones.
With two of them he twisted the stag's horns,
and had a pair of thyrsi ready made.

The third he bent and made a sacred wreath
and with it garlanded his human brows
where, swollen with the effort still, his veins
were gloomy with the blood that burned beneath.

So wreathed, and armed with his two Bacchic rods,
he raised his giant mouth towards the Sky
to breathe once more. He heard the distant Sea
echoing with its roar the murmuring woods.

Only one Cloud was in the highest height,
as 'twere a goddess half-undressed for sleep.
The Offspring of the Cloud revered that shape
Ixion had the nerve to fecundate.

Such liveliness as no one has been able
to vie with yet coursed through his limbs. He reared
up suddenly. The fleeting Shadow made
for twilight gloom and made itself a Fable.

148

# The asphodel

GLAUCO

Derbe, an asphodel is washed ashore!
Whoever can have picked and offered it
to wander like a sea-flower on the wave?

O Derbe, think how many flowers will bloom
unseen by us, way up the tawny mountains!
Along the sounding banks of curving rivers!

How many in a thousand unknown regions
which yet have their own names as flowers do,
names that are wild and rough and fresh and soft,

names whence the exile's heart derives some pain
because the well-known sounds send up a scent
as leaves of sage do to the man who bites them!

DERBE

But I know where the asphodel will bloom.
There in the bright Mugello, near to Giogo
di Scarperia, I saw it flowering white.

I even saw it, Glauco, and I picked it,
upon that mountain known as Catenaia;
on Uccellina too near Alberese,

there in the pale Maremma where perhaps
it smiles at Hades' image in the very
instant it dies beneath the horse's hoof.

GLAUCO

And I too, Derbe, wandering in the footsteps
of the lethean lady, saw in bloom,
from Populonia to the Argentaro,

the clematis. All the white sisters held
the rugged woodland in the silence in
delicate arms, and the black ilexes

149

and knotty cork-trees in the sun of June
were sound asleep like venerable heroes
behind the white veils of their youthful brides.

### DERBE

In Populonia very rich in elders
I got to know the hoarhound which must take
the musky scent it has from spotted serpents,

and the dwarf elder with its berries used
to colour wine, and rushes used to cover
the swollen glass in which the wine matures.

### GLAUCO

The honeysuckle, like the clematis
softening with its breath the roughest boles,
I saw by the Fegana at Tereglio,

I saw the reed adorning Marinella
di Luni, and on mountains of La Verna
the flowering ash weave coronals for May.

### DERBE

The red and yellow lilies of the mountains
I saw too, at Frattetta under Sagro,
at Cisa too in Lunigiana, and

on Mommio where, in the remotest sky,
I heard the eagle scream. The lilies seemed
immortal spirits in the eternal circle.

Those places were attractive, but so wild
they seemed to be a sword piercing my breast.
I touched, and with a lily, the great rock

which did not open and which did not tremble.
And yet there seemed a miracle performed,
O Glauco, for I went on like a god.

### GLAUCO

Mouth of the Serchio, where the sandy plain
is scribbled on obscurely with the tracks
of crows which make their signs seem sibylline:

150

I picked the lily of a day, the while
the south was bending the salt tamarisks,
bright cypresses beside the bitter wave.

I knew the Attic smilax; and at Gombo
I also knew the lily which is called
pancrazio, name most dear to Grecian youth;

it seemed to me so white with purity
that to the Manes of the sky-blue Orpheus,
to the Cor cordium, I offered it.


DERBE

We made, O Glauco, from the Earth itself
the woman loved, and every most occluded
grace we have had from her through strength of love.

When the Sun enters in the balanced Scales,
I shall conduct you on the heights of Pieve
di Camaiore, to Tambura also,

the Frigido's clear springs, by the Freddana
beyond Forci, and to Soraggio's Mount,
that you may see the flowering of the gentian.


GLAUCO

The Earth is bright, O Derbe, and to us
most dear. But oh how many flowers will bloom
unseen by us, in valleys full of salt!

The Oceanids will decorate with garlands
the edges of her dress where Demeter
is mourning for the saffron's apparition.

When the Sun enters into Scorpio, Derbe,
I shall conduct you on high Giovo's pastures
and in among the flocks of fattening clouds,

that you may see the flowering of the saffron.

151

# Summer madrigals

## Supplication

Summer, my Summer, please do not decline!
But sooner let this heart of mine explode,
a pomegranate burst by too much heat.

Summer, Summer, be slow to ripen vine-
clusters upon the poplars where they're trained.
And let the saffron bloom a little late.

Hold closely up against your sturdy chest
subtle September, lest he go too fast.

Suffocate, Summer, in between your breasts
this maker of baskets and vats where grapes are pressed.

## The sands of Time

With fine warm sand continually on the run
out of the hollow of the idle hand,
the heart could see the days were drawing in.

The heart was struck with sudden anxious fear,
the humid equinox being close at hand
which dims the gold upon the salty shore.

This hand a vessel for the sands of Time,
this palpitating heart an hourglass, while
the shadow lengthened from each empty stem –
shades of the needle on the silent dial!

## The footprint

The sun was getting low. Along the coast
I reached the lazy mouth of the Motrone
and bared my feet that I might wade across.

From a migrating troop a clarion blast
came through the air to join the deep sea moaning.
A wild horse neighed from the esparto grass.

I stopped. A footprint in the mud was strange.
But shades were falling from the mountain range.


### At dawn

At dawn I saw once more at that same spot
that print most like the footprint of a fawn;
except I noticed that there were five toes.

I saw the big toe somewhat set apart
from the others and the little toe withdrawn –
exactly like the oystercatcher's claws.

The blocked-up river-mouth (such black bits there!)
gave off a scent of salt and juniper.

Like hound or setter sniffing out a bay
roebuck, I followed after the faint print.
I reached the reeds and found the hedgehog there.

A livid grass-snake slid through weeds away.
Already of a rather yellowish tint,
two or three chaffinches took to the air.

I noticed something white – a veil of dawn.
The trail was lost through gazing at the dawn.


### At midday

At midday I discovered in the reeds
of the Motrone's clay the savage nymph,
the black-lashed one, the sister of Syrinx.

153

And then I had her on my sylvan knees;
I savoured her saliva's taste and scent –
the pungency of marjoram and mint.

Across the thunder of our loving ardour
we heard the crackle on the reedy bed
of August rain which was as warm as blood.

Upon the parched and brown baked clay we heard
the trembling of a thousand mouths – our thirst.

### *Towards evening*

I go towards evening to the glade. I capture
the filly in a noose. She is still wild.
Between her teeth she still has foam of pasture.

I grip the bare back like a pair of pincers;
and underneath her arms I grasp my naiad,
and lift her up, and set her on the withers.

With bark and branch beneath the plunging hooves
the mass of cones and needles spirts and splashes.
Beyond the dykes, a triform tangle moves
over the tawny stubble where it flashes!

### *Circean charm*

Between the two ports, and between their beacons,
dead calm without a mist without a cloud,
calm water lightly veined like your pale temples.

Not near at all, beyond the Argentaro,
not near at all the rocks and swampy land
of Circe, goddess of the many herbs.

And she has charmed for us with juice of herbs
the Tyrrhene Sea like one enormous cauldron!

## The wind writes

The wind is writing on the soft sand here
with wing-feathers for quills; and in his language
the signs speak out along the white seashore.

But, when the sun declines, from every mark
a shadow is created, from each ripple,
as from eyelashes on the smoothest cheek.

It seems that on the shore's wide empty face
your smile is multiplied a thousand ways.

## Sea-lanterns

The jellyfish are luminous like dim
lanterns along the Syren's fabled course
where pale roots and sea-lettuces are spread.

Over the whitened shores there breathes a calm,
and the full moon, arising now, can scarce
show where salt tamarisks are throwing shade.

The suck of feeble lips is made by water
filling the print left by your gentle foot.

## In the slime

Now in their slime the rushes have the odour
of peaches almost rotten and of roses
that shrivel, of spoilt honey, and of death.

155

Now all the marish seems to be a flower
made out of mud the sun of August scorches,
with who knows what sweet stuffiness of death.

The frog is dumb, when I am near at hand.
The gaseous bubbles rise without a sound.

*The Grecian grape*

Down in Achaea now a certain Greek
grape clustered like the curls of Hyacinth
is baking, and already turning black.

That is the grape they call the passolina,
down on the isthmus too, and in Corinth,
and on that island white with doves – Aegina.

Onchestus, where my bunch of grapes was blue
as tail of swallow like a fork in flight!
It was within the shade of Neptune's tomb
I savoured it, with Helicon in sight.

## August festival

Hesperus gushes like a trembling tear
on Val di Magra whence slow vapour fumes.
In the extinguished sky down over there
one last peak flames.

In competition with that star that peak
the light on Lighthouse Island shines the winner.
Meanwhile Cape Crow is doubled by a brig
and by a schooner.

Rosin and floating weeds from time to time
mix in the wind that blows from ocean waste.
The scenting pinewood takes from bitter brine
a salty taste.

The sea is white, with shining crystalline
streaks, and its breath is hardly heard on land.
The Cape is softened and its sharp outline
crumbles like sand.

Everything seems to want to be less hard.
Uranian peace wraps all things up down here.
Even steep rocky Pania's getting blurred
in the soft air.

Youngster, hang garlands on the architrave;
melt wax to fix the pipes which sound so shrill;
top up the lamp once more with Buti's smooth
and flowing oil.

Shout for your friends who play upon the reeds
that they may gather with us in a hurry
bringing their syrinxes from broad reed-beds
round Camaiore.

Bring seven torches of the scented pine
and seven of the prickly juniper,
that they throughout the wood for those who come
make the way clear.

There will be treats for all to pick and choose
arranged in order on the cleanly mat:
grapes grown in the Five Regions full of juice,
the black the white,

with figs and peaches on the gleaming mat,
and all with leaves and tendrils of the vine,
and Calci olives, sweetest of the sweet,
pickled in brine.

May mullet redden on our low straw table
among the carp-like dentex and umbrina,
wine from Vernazza in its bulging bottle,
wine from Corniglia.

We shall enjoy that flour and honey cake
so grateful to the lustful garden god,
with garlands bulrush and white poplar make
for every head.

Youngsters, we shall be kind to you as well.
As I arrange it you will not forget
my August feast, so but sweet music shrill
from every flute.

Then light the torches up, and let us go
into the wood to guide the coming guest.
I hear the ringing laugh of one I know,
one I know best.

Yes this is she who stirs my spirits so,
whose bitter laughter makes her language sweeter.
Through myrtles with lit torches let us go
some way to meet her.

Nor wonder if the saffron robe, so stately,
seem current by the Serchio and the Magra.
This guest in fact is a Boeotian lady,
and from Tanagra.

The grace with which she girds the yellow lawn,
showing her sandalled feet, is wonderful
(see crystal rings and amber rings upon
her ankles) while

her head of subtly interwoven hair
bends over, and a long pin holds the plaits,
hair tawny red like seaside juniper
the north-west bites.

Sweet-scented juniper roars in the tead.
Now fix the lighted stick into the ground.
To you, wild flutes, oh may the god concede
harmonious sound.

Pan shield us from a note that's faint or bitter.
Play well together, youngsters. Take good care!
This guest who hears you has, being from Tanagra,
an excellent ear.

# The many-headed song

Snap all the flutes. The linen that connects
their reeds is that same linen used for wily
snares, and the wax has too much taste of honey.

The childish sound makes but a brief oblivion
for the outstanding man who does not love
to fool about or snatch at a chance of sleep.

You're not the citizen of Agrigento
named Midas, victor in the Delphic games.
Nor were you taught by Pallas the great song.

Pallas Athene with the firm blue eyes
first found that song, that day she found Medusa
decapitated by the sickle sword.

She heard the loud laments that Euryala
emitted through the hissing of her serpents
towards the kill; she heard the hideous plaint.

The groans of Stheno were like arrows piercing
the ether, and all of the uprearing snakes
were menacing the hero born from gold.

And so the Thousand-Headed Melody
was born on a day of blood; and blue-eyed Pallas
gathered it up to modulate for man.

The reeds of the reed-beds of Orchomenus
she trimmed and garnished with thin plates of bronze,
and so she made the tone more powerful.

Snap your exiguous flutes, you callow flautists,
since they're too weak to manage the great song.
Find for me in the sea the twisted shells.

I shall instruct you face to face with tempests
to draw out from the enormous twisted trumpets
the melody of a thousand fates, my fates.

# Triton

Triton was my instructor and my lord.
He squats upon the seasand where the spume
bubbles; the sun causes his scales to fume.
I rise to where the fish becomes the god:

his massive breast is blue as dyer's woad
but on his back the silver makes him gleam.
He chooses from the algae the most green,
and ruminates; he dribbles salty weed.

He seizes on his shell with vast webbed hand,
blowing hard into it as he is used
with swollen neck and cheeks and twisty-eyed.

The sound re-echoes over sea and land.
Mount Luni staggers, stricken with the blast.
I feel the dithyrambs leap up inside.

# Roman sarcophagus

And where, Mount Luni, are the statues now?
Today my spirits struggle to survive
in symbols standing out against the sky.

O ancient marbles in great Roman gardens!
They loom the length of steps and balusters
and loggias in their tunics of green moss.

Cypresses ilexes and box-trees blacken
about the fountain's edge where Silence with a
finger upon his lips bends to the mirror.

He sees appearing from the depths a skull –
Medusa's, the Gorgonian – and he sees
himself fixed in the horror of her gaze.

Fates are lamented in the peacock's cry.
All is finished in stone: life that is dead,
graves with grave memories, unending shade.

I pick out a sarcophagus, one sculptured
on three sides with a battling Alexander;
earth it contains now, and an oleander.

There I shall chew on my own laurel-tree's
harsh leaf, sitting on that sarcophagus.

There pluck the petals from my empty rose
of love, sitting on that sarcophagus.

# Ocean laurel

Apollo's plant, ambiguous oleander,
with that sweet smell at evening amber makes;
pomegranate, who sprout your red balausta
flamelike inside a calyx all of wax;

scaly-trunked pine familiar to the sailor,
with hidden cones within your thickest locks;
olive contorted by some old neuralgia,
with fruit that blackens; juniper that pricks,

heart-warming myrtle crackling in the heat,
terebinth, honeysuckle, mastic tree,
a hundred wreaths of Summer in Ausonia;

but, ocean laurel, you I also need,
who give your name to the Sargasso Sea,
black-berried like the laurel of Aonia.

# The prisoner

Ardi – sad as the naked Prisoner
sculptured by mighty Michelangelo
out of what gleams untrodden and remote,
Mount Sagro, for the pontiff who made war –

you too are straitened by your own obscure
lot, victim for the Sea of the Unknown;
with silent mouth wide open to complain
against the doom that took away your power.

Were you once Gela's tyrant, whose success
the Pythian lauded? And did you enslave
from Thespia men and marbles for your home

in Thebes? Or did you ride on your white horse
with Pericles' great father to achieve
Mycale's victory in Hebe's name?

# The Victory of Samothrace

If she, whose spreading wings both arm and honour
that trireme's prow sailing from Samothrace,
is speeding now to me who know no peace
persisting with my twice-ten-years' hard labour,

nowhere but here where masts and yard-arms prosper,
this coastal pine-wood born of summer's blaze
below the solid Alp whose silent face
is glorious in its everlasting candour,

shall I give greeting: 'You are right to come
here from that shore which hosts the Càbiri,
here from that isle against the Hebrus River.

The Greeks acknowledge me their latest son:
I sucked the dugs of all antiquity;
and still a fiery daemon makes me quiver.'

# The rupestrian peplos

Wingèd goddess, cut short at arms and neck,
you rule the crest of Mount Altissimo.
Apollo's white-haired augur long ago
went down to Stygian darkness through your rock.

This rugged mountain never known to shake
portrays your peplos, Nike, when it's blown
back by the wind! You leave where you have been
traces which animate the stony peak.

When sea near Luni at the close of day
flames and Ceràgiola is red as blood
beneath Altissimo's subjecting height,

then blazing out of rock you break away
and I feel fall like rain upon my head
the pelting joy of your impetuous flight.

# The vulture of the Sun

When at odd times I ponder, and regard
the salt air flickering, a sheet of flame,
and in the silence hear the falling pine
's dull thud, the resin spluttering in the tead,

the flautist of the marsh sound from his mud,
the sedge and millet still at their dry din,
then suddenly you seize this heart of mine,
you prey upon me trembling and afraid,

O Glory, Glory, vulture of the Sun,
who swoop on me and grasp me in your claws
even on this hot seashore where I hide!

I raise my face, although my heart is down,
and through the redness of the eyes I close
I see a world resplendent in my blood.

# The wing on the sea

Ardi, upon the sea one wing alone,
a faded bit of wreckage, floats around.
Its feathers, since they are no longer bound,
tremble at every breath of wind that's blown.

Ardi, I see the wax! That wing is one
the author of the wooden cow designed,
one wing of Icarus, made in the land
of Minos where the filthy deed was done.

Who will gather it up? Now which of us
can join the scattered plumes and bind them tight,
attempting that mad exploit once again?

Oh high fate of the son of Daedalus!
That hero ventured with no middle flight,
and fell into the ocean all alone.

## Altius egit iter

The shade of Icarus is still at large
in hot Mediterranean gulfs and harbours.
It tracks that vessel's wake which foams the most.
It equals in its speed the strongest gale.
It loves man's voice commanding in the whirlwind.
It hears the constant cry of shipwrecked sailors
and holds it in disdain, because that shadow's
fall was as silent as it was remote.

I saw it over there, towards the sunset.
Then I was in my pinnace at the oars,
my Lord my daemon sitting at the prow,
regarding fixedly my secret care.
I saw between us two quite suddenly
the naked shade of Icarus appear.
It almost seemed the colour of the sea
had tinged his limbs, and yet his eyes were sunlit.

The two red zones or bands were still in place,
fixed crosswise on his adolescent breast,
over his shoulders for the wings of course,
like crimson baldrics where no weapons hung.
'O Lord, this shadow is,' I said, 'my ancient
brother. My joy is to renew his ventures
in the unknown. Indulge, O Unsubdued,
this greed which takes me to the heights and depths.'

# Fourth dithyramb

Icarus said: 'The daughter of the Sun
stood leaning on me as I were a sapling
marking the meadow's edge
and gazed towards the candid herd of cattle
that grazed along the rocky Cèrato.
My right shoulder was low
under the pressure of her regal hand
wet with an icy sweat; and, deep inside
me, I was trembling to the very core,
a great noise in my ears
ringing so loudly that I was afraid
I heard from sacred Dicte the atrocious
Corybantes and the clashing bronze they beat.
Knossos was shining out,
that city walled with bricks and blocks of stone
beyond the rough reed-bed whence darts are cut.
"What are you gazing at?"
the King asked Pasiphae. He came up panting
heavily through a beard as violet
as Cretan grapes; for he was strongly built,
his hips exorbitant with yellow fat.
"I'm looking at the white
bull which you did not offer to Poseidon"
the daughter of Perseis made reply.
And the snow-covered heights
of Ida were less white than was that bull
denied to the deep god and white as snow.
"Why do you tremble so,
Daedalus' son?" the King demanded then.
Pasiphae answered: "This Athenian
youth brings Androgeos back into my mind,
him who did not return:
and that is why I lean
on him for my support;
and that is why it is sweet
to run my fingers through his prolix mane."
I saw Ilissus again,
the plane-trees laurels and the oleanders

170

which overshadow it, Colonus' grove
of olives grateful to the nightingale.
I saw my native soil
once more flash suddenly across my mind,
which happens to the one whose end is near;
as through my mane of hair
the solar lady ran her fingering hand,
it seemed that my bones burned,
in her smile's ardour which was oh so close,
like branches where a flame is clinging tight:
Summer has dried them out
and with its rich aroma they are rich.
And all of the curved ships
with all the oarsmen sitting at the rowlocks
seated in lines to strike the cloven flood,
Eracleos, Amnisus,
those curving ports, the river, and the mountains,
and everything upon the woody island,
with vineyards with the dittany with honey,
as burning in that smile
I saw between my slowly closing lids.
And the leader of the herds
I could hear lowing in the crackling blaze:
again the white bull lows,
the bull that was refused to the Earthshaker.'

Icarus said: 'Soon as the shadows fell
(the isolated summit of Mount Ida
was reddened in the ether,
red as the spiky dittany in flower)
I went back to the meadows secretly,
my silent heart swollen with hate; I hurled
hard at the bull some jagged lumps of flint
torn from that river-bed
(the Cèrato) and loaded in my sling.
And then the herdsman heard
me and he chased me swiftly through the grasses
shaking the menace of his hazel-rod.
But in the deepening shade
he lost all trace of me; he did not know me,

171

nor did the grass serve to preserve my prints.
Unutterable sense
of wicked lust was everywhere! It quivered
even in wandering stars, or so it seemed!
It seemed the sudden wind
opened up bitter wounds in my bare body,
and bitter as there would have been no power
to heal in all of Ida's dittany.
And many a wretched cry
was strangled in my throat in that great heat.
Then I came to the walls
of the great Labyrinth my cunning father,
amazing in his ways and his delays,
filled with intelligent laborious error.
There I stayed still and hidden
because I saw the strong sure craftsman standing
in silence on the complicated threshold
and the Sun's daughter in great secrecy
there talking with him and without a smile,
her face marmoreal,
as one requiring from his mortal art
some dreadful thing she did not tremble at.'

Icarus said: 'My father's secret smithy
was in a garden with a view of curving
Eracleos all crowded
with well-constructed hulls and brightly painted
prows; and the craftsman's tools were very sharp,
the craftsman's forehead closely wrinkled up.
There rose the very shape
of the deceptive cow into the light
of day, as though, being surfeited with pasture,
she breathed out of her nostrils scented breath,
lucerne's sweet breath, calm on her cloven feet.
The wood was shaped and put
together with such art and covered over
with such fresh hide the creature's side seemed blessed
with a fertility that could not fail
with udders on the point of swelling up
because a sudden flow of milk had come.

172

Into the garden came
the furtive Pasiphae without her ladies
to gaze in admiration at the work
it seemed she was inflaming with her own
impatient lust; and with her came the shaggy
herdsman who made the perfect judge for her.
He laughed, because he saw
a defect in the dewlap. The great workman
bowed to the boor's opinion then and there.
Pasiphae, with her bare
arms pressing down upon my naked shoulders,
let herself go on me as on a senseless
fulcrum, sunk as she was in her inhuman
dream, and lost in her love's monstrosity.
There rose a violent fire
out of the very soil where I had rooted
my strength, and it completely wrapped me up,
and as it were the rosin from a shrub
it seemed to crackle all around and shine.
Oh garden with such fine
aromas, laden with such wax and honey,
laden with resinous gum as gold as amber,
where one might hear the pomegranate burst
and burst out like an unexpected laugh
dissolving must-like in a golden mouth!
There came upon the South
the singing of the maids in the remote
palace, those who were sitting at the loom
those dyeing various wools in tints of purple
those for infusions picking simples out
and those preparing meals of chosen meat
for the daughter of the Sun,
not knowing that she was before the Sun
a slavering prey to monstrous Aphrodite.'

Icarus said: 'The daughter of the Sun
I loved, she who submitted out of lust
to what was after all the best-hung beast.
Oh, how her substance glittered
godlike, the first time that she went inside

173

the cunning effigy and was embruted.
Inside myself I burned.
I, when I saw the sly and wily herdsman
that first time leading up
to the pretended heifer the white bull
which beat its sounding tail
against its side as though it were a whip,
its short horns decorated with a strip
of red, I started with a cry: "O Sun,
I shall today to you, up on the solid
rock, consecrate an eagle a high-flyer!"
And I went higher and higher,
with arrows bow and axe, with cothurns on,
to make my best amends for what I had done.'

He said: 'At first I saw the enormous shadow
quivering on the hot and stony ground.
The rock was tawny and sky-blue the shadow.
And then I heard the sound
made by the wings upon the stricken air.
She screamed against her fate,
suspended for one moment on slow wings;
my bowstring as I tugged at it called out:
the bird's scream seemed to lacerate the sky
and the string's call was gentle as the chirp
of swallows but the bolt
that flew from it was strong and dangerous.
I felt upon my face
the wind made by the bird trying to rise;
she lost her strength, went whirling in a gyre,
then dropped down on the mountainside like lead.
There fell upon my head
one hot and heavy drop, a drop of blood,
most like the drop that leaves an August cloud
with flash and thunderstone.
The eagle struck the rock, her breast was prone,
her splendid wings were spread
making a dreadful noise against the rock,
and sudden in defence she raised her beak.
Now the precipitous rock

was burning in the heat of noon like iron
inside a furnace, underneath my cothurns.
The frond of the viburnum
was coloured greyish brown like dross of molten
metal, as was the flowering ash's frond.
Capricorns could be heard
bleating among the spiky dittany,
while from the vulnerary herb there rose
a scent upon the air
to mingle with the scent of eagle's blood
which is vermilion more than other blood.
With its claws and its beak
this bird, Jove's follower, was prompt to fight
against the huntsman who had wounded it
upon the solid rock.
And then I said: "High-flyer,
you cannot fly; I have no weapons either."
For I would not retreat
and from a place of safety shoot at it.
I threw my bow away; I bound about
my hand the well-tooled leather from my quiver,
bound my right hand about
to hold before my eyes against the threat
of the hooked beak. I ran against it, entered
into a savage shuddering of feathers;
into the dreadful clamour of those feathers
as in a tawny whirlwind I was taken
by the rapacious will;
I felt the rock slip underneath my heel
and shouted a great shout.
It was in a dull roar of death we fought.
With my right hand I seized it by the throat,
as strong and thick as is a serpent's trunk,
and squeezed and squeezed; and with my left I drew
my first dart from the freshly bleeding wound,
then plunged it deeper in
again and yet again.
We struggled on the edge of the abyss,
at midday, in the presence of the Sun.
Glory of Icarus!

175

Each flutter of the feathers in the brawl
spirted a thousand drops
of blood like purple set alight in sparks
and flying off in fervent festival.
My head in celebration
seemed to be crowned all round with all these sparks.
And feathers from the spurs
from underneath the wings from breast from neck
flew off upon the South.
Also a crimson streamlet from the beak
went flowing down along all my empurpled
arm to the elbow. Torn by all these blows
these claws my right side was so bloodied over
Nike the messenger,
if she perhaps delayed upon the lonely
peak on her way towards my native Athens
bringing with her the crown
made of wild olive, made comparison
between the eagle's and Icarian blood.
I did not fear the judgement of the Sun.
It seemed, when I relaxed my hostile grip
with my opponent sprawling on the rock
spent at the last, it seemed to me that all
the ability to fly had been transfused
into these very arms these very shoulders
and now was rousing in my inmost heart
an inextinguishable greed for flight.
Only the towering peak
and my exanimate prey were with me there,
and the god who guides the chariot of light.
I prayed: "O charioteer,
I offer up to you this sacrifice
to beg your patronage
if it be given me to tempt the ways
where you shake out your horses' candid manes.
The breast the entrails and the branching claws
and the immense beaked head
I burn in one enormous brushwood blaze,
also the lethal reed.
Grant, O majestic god, if you hear me,

176

grant me that I from out the burning embers
may snatch the eagle's mighty wings away
and take them off with me
so that they may be studied by my father,
my father Daedalus
of Athens, that most skilful artisan,
and so that he, that man of many wiles,
may make two like them but much stronger even
and made up of a greater mass of feathers."
I took my axe in hand
which had been hanging from my belt behind:
with it I hacked into the eagle's joints
which were so tough with tendons and with muscle
that they resisted all the axe's blows.
"Oh, that anvil and hammer
and all my father's work will not suffice
to plant in me the virtue of the wings
up on my collar-bone" I thought to myself,
seeing, as though I were a cithara-player
leaning over the strings,
just how tenacious was the sinewy joint
which showed up gleaming white, colour of pearl,
in all that blood. And so my mind was sad.
The amputated wing was a sad sight.
And, with the flesh left over for the Sun
smoking upon a fire of brushwood, I
thought to myself: "The god,
alone upon his shining car, is sorry,
careless of the unwonted sacrifice.
His daughter in the shameful effigy
is what he sees, all-seeing;
he is tormented by Daedalian art
and opens the sore wound inside my heart,
my uncomplaining heart
not dittany nor other herb can heal."
I lifted up both wings
joined with the leather fastening of my belt;
and will-power went along as the companion
of inescapable grief
when, guided by the god, and stained with blood,

177

I went down from the mountain to the Maze.'

Icarus said: 'My father's secret smithy
was in a cavern of the precipice
behind Amnisus, to
the east of Knossos, lonely on the sea.
Here could be heard the screams
and squawkings of the sea-birds endlessly
from caverns in the rusty-coloured cliff.
The sandstone ground was thick
with scraps of ancient pitchers scattered round
and heaps of whitish dung.
The hollow walls of the cave
redounded sound to Iapyx, salt north-west,
as though the curving shields of the Curetes
under the furious beating of the pikes.
Below, the din of waves
echoed through all the windings of the caves
whenever Apheliotes
inflated blue-green goatskins in the salt.
And there my father was,
intent on his unnatural task, and there
without anvil or hammer
he worked to put the means of flight together.
Truly I caused him care
and trouble, for it always seemed to me
his work was lagging well behind desire;
it always seemed the feathers were too few
which he had put together as he worked.
For him the golden wax,
rolled into balls, with hot breath and with thumb
I softened; and I plucked the plenteous game;
I took great care to pick the feathers out
separate from the down.
The blood which gathered beaded at the tip
of every quill I plucked
seemed to me full of potency; I liked
to suck it all out drop by drop, while crouching
close by the industrious man of miracles
who sat upon a stone.

178

How many times I emptied my whole quiver,
unwearied wandering sagittarius
among the distant rocks!
So many falcons sparrow-hawks and buzzards
dropped dead, so many bald
vultures encumbered with their carrion flesh,
and goshawks with remains of colubers
still in their hooked beaks, and Strymonian cranes,
long-legged, with those slim bones
the flautist finds so useful, every kind
full-feathered and high-flying dropped down dead
struck by the vigour of my Cretan bow
and reedy Cretan darts.
And then I came back laden with celestial
booty back to the cave;
and still it always seemed to my desire
my father's work was all too slow by far.
Inside there always was the scent of wax
mixed with the scent of resin, for the workman
was mingling in the opalescent tear
the pine sheds with the bee's malleable gift
to give that even more tenacity.
He had excluded metals from the gear
because they are too heavy; and the framework,
the skeleton, was made up out of strong
flexible rods of hazel, held together
with twisted thread in hard invisible knots,
and he had stretched right over it the caul,
the fatty net or membrane which contains
an animal's intestines, well dried out.
And on this apparatus, strong and light,
he fixed the feathers in their proper order,
from the most short up to the longest, chosen
with accuracy out, as in the pipes
of Pan the disparate oats are shaded off
to give the different notes that are required.
And he used flax and wax to join them up,
wax mixed with rosin, as I said before.
And he knew how to bend them with such art
to reproduce, and to the very life,

179

the curvature of wings, so that a wing
unmoving on the rock seemed warm and vibrant
and lifted by the windy air, as though
upon the point of bursting from the nest
or on the point of settling after flight.'

Icarus said: 'Although not seen, I saw.
I ventured with my eyes inside a rose-bush,
where at my very breath without a sound
two or three withered roses lost their petals.
It seemed that with them too
my heart broke up and fell upon the ground.
And bitter endlessly
was everything I saw, although not seen,
in that mute garden where
thick resin was no longer heard to pour
lamenting or the pomegranate burst
all of a sudden with its bright red laugh.
The fruits were soft and rotten,
and wrinkled up like dried-out strips of leather;
the trees, dry rugged sticks;
the sweet cells of the honey-bee, dry sponges,
without the sound of working melody.
Broken upon the ground,
eaten into, shapeless, a wretched carcase,
was the notorious cow
offered deceptively to the white bull
so that the famous side
of the daughter of the Sun
be filled through that device with bestial seed.
And then the royal lady,
child of the Sun and of the Oceanid,
Pasiphae child of Perseis, whose face
appeared to me more brilliant than the light
in the Sun's temple's innermost recess,
the queen of the famed isle,
that cradle for the newborn son of Chronos
rich in dittany grapes honey and darts,
the adulteress of the grazing grounds was there,
alone with all her fear.

180

Her mouth was panting, nostrils sour, her eyes
intent, her face as pallid as dried grass,
used up, beaded with sweat
and flakes of foam, the residue of lust.
She was half-naked and,
her hair being all unkempt, she looked half wild,
as though a woman of a Bacchic band
who worn with orgies shudders in a ditch
on Cithaeron, death-pale,
the thyrsus reft of foliage and the skin
of wine, caught in the cold before the dawn.
She felt inside her belly, shuddering,
the dreadful monster quicken,
her son, a bovine but a human thing.'

Icarus said: 'The sky was full of stars,
the sea was full of peace,
through all of that miraculous watch of mine,
while the red star within
my watchful heart shone brightest of them all.
And all those pitiful
things were far off from me as though I were
a god who flown with nectar walks on air.
It seemed from my lithe body
the mournful burden disappeared just as
from eastern skies the shades were disappearing;
my disencumbered flesh
was radiated with light airy blood.
The eastern sky was lit
in twilight, and the brilliant messenger
of Dawn caused over the expanse of waters
a never-ending trembling to appear.
Then suddenly the laughter of the sea
was changed into tumultuous desire
and bristling with innumerable scales.
And then it seemed that flames
that make the day were born inside my heart;
for ever there had set
behind me all the stars which shine at night;
for me the wings of fate

181

were spread already for the dangerous flight.
Oh, on the passive stone
the apparatus lay exanimate,
and my too-human arms were stripped quite bare
of wings and all the power
my axe upon the mount had cut away
that day of victory.
And suddenly there came into my mind
just how tenacious was the sinewy joint
which showed up gleaming white, colour of pearl,
in all that crimson blood.
"Conquering eagle" I said "Icarus, son
of the Athenian,
consecrates to your shade these delicate
and artificial means of soaring flight
which are the work of man;
because, just as he conquered you in fight
both far and near, so too in your domain
he wishes to excel in dash and daring."
I roused my father from his sleep. I said:
"Father, it's time." I said no more. I stood
silent while he arranged the wings upon
my shoulders, and while he reiterated
his words of warning with uncertain voice.
"You need to fly along the middle way;
if you fly low, the water will weigh down
your wings; if you fly up too high, the fire
will burn. Keep always to the golden mean.
Take me as leader; follow in my wake.
And oh, my son, do not be overbold.
I shall mark out the path. You follow me."
And as he spoke his skilful hands were trembling.
I held the marvellous workman in complete
silent contempt. And "When the flight begins
I shall be struggling hard to overcome you.
From the first wing-beat I shall be your rival,
employing all my strength to overcome you.
And my road will be everywhere, deep down,
high up, in water, fire, in flood, in cloud,
yes everywhere except the middle way;

182

and never in your wake, though I be lost"
this heart of mine replied to him in silence.
Back to my mind there came the great deceit
(I found forgetfulness so difficult
that even Lethe's water did not give it,
not even though three cups had been gulped down)
and well-wrought fraud came back into my mind.
And in his skilful hands that still were trembling
I seemed to see once more the sharpened tools
working to gratify the desperate wish.
"Icarus, do you hear? I shall rise first,
and not impetuously. And you must follow."
But with an eagle's art I took to flight,
and flew up from the threshold of our cavern
so forcefully that we were separated
at once. The flocks of birds rose up in strident
panic from the red rocks in front of me,
and fearing my attack they disappeared.
Freedom at last! I felt the morning air
pelt through my naked body, all its coolness
flow through me with refreshing clarity:
not even the torrents where I used to wash
away the blood and dust after the hunt
had ever drenched me in such deep delight.
Oh in my heart the swiftness of the beat
which in its steady rhythm powered my flight!
I felt the baldrics crossed upon my breast
changing already into binding tendons,
all of the circumambient azure pouring
into my lungs, the firmament resplendent
upon my breast as on the terrible
breast of great Pan. "Icarus! Icarus!"
my distant father shouted. "Icarus!"
In the wind and in the rush from time to time
his cry came to my ears, from time to time
my name as it was called out by his fear
came to me in impetuous delight.
"Icarus!" And the cry was not so loud.
"Icarus!" For the final time. Alone,
alone and winged in the immensity!

I passed into the bosom of a cloud:
inside there was a warmth, a sweet and strange
perfume, as though Nephele's breath, the mother
of her who gave the Hellespont its name.
The wind made by the flapping wings deranged
their delicate layers, revealing something reddish
and something white. A sweet and strange perfume
was making me feel feeble, my wings damp.
Then I began to drop. I saw eleven
ships, blue-prowed ships, furnished with polished decks,
ships which beat at the sea with blades of oars
in slow and steady harmony of strokes,
moving to distant ventures. On the bridge
crescent-shaped shields were shining and round shields
made out of bronze, long spears. There came to me
the sailors' shouts. And I flew on at speed
and overtook them. What was in the minds
of those rough men who saw that prodigy?
How did they speak of me? Perhaps they said:
"Upon a field of carnage the intrepid
Nike, within the shade of a high pile
of overturned and broken chariots,
or by a trophy of illustrious arms,
on bloody earth submitted to the hero
who seized her by the hair: he made her pregnant.
This youth who wings his way with such strong wings
up there will no doubt be the child she had."
High-hearted I was pleased to hear such words,
although imagined, for like Nike's son
I wanted to be seen to roar and rage.
And down there far below on sculptured Paros
I saw shine out the candour of Marpessos.
And then I saw from Delos, wandering isle,
the smoke of spotless hecatombs arise.
Then I saw nothing more, except the Sun.
Then nothing more I wanted, but to see
him close to, standing in his burning car,
to reach him, and to dare
to seize that horse's reins upon the left,
Aethon that horse with nostrils flaming red.

Having achieved the head-
gear and the boots with wings that Hermes wears
in my noon dream, I was delirious.
Conjoined with Sirius,
the Sun who is resplendent far and wide
was at the culmination of the sky.
And I was yearning for
the height so hard to reach, the terrible heat,
to offer him the wings which back in Crete
I had excluded from the holocaust.
My strength was not exhaust,
or so it seemed to me, while my mind moved
the lifeless feathers, my immortal mind
moved them and not brief arms.
Then something slight a very delicate shadow
I saw beneath me in the depths of light,
down there where there appeared no trace at all
of the dim sea or of the dusky earth;
I saw another shadow, then another.
I said. "My time has come."
There was no lack of heart. I did not shout
against my fate, like that bird consecrate
to die beneath the arrow I had shot;
my father's warning I did not regret.
I looked down fearlessly;
I saw those delicate shadows were the feathers
out of my wings, and they were fluttering down
free from the softened wax.
I raised myself then with a surge of life
towards the Sun: I heard the chariot wheels
rumble above my risen head; I heard
the horses' fourfold trample; saw the sparks
flash from the golden axle, panting fire
breathe from the horses, Pirois with mane
uplift, and Aethon with the scarlet nostrils.
The horses of the Sun
whinnied as one. And Phlegon's gleaming belly
was yellow-green like chrysolite; the foam
from Eos shone out like the veil of Iris.
I saw the fist that clenched

to hold the reins, I heard the stinging whip
whistle above the fire. I stretched my arms.
I cried "O Sun!" That face
that cannot be described, beneath the hair
dripping ambrosia, turned and bent to me;
its rays around it made a thousand crowns.
"Son of Hyperion,
Icarus offers up to you these man-
made wings unseen before
which had the power to rise right up to You!"
The wheels with their great rumble swallowed up
my voice which was not begging from the god
pity but lasting praise.
And wheeling round through everlasting light
I fell into this deep Sea which is mine.'

Icarus, Icarus, into the depths
I pray I may sink too, and be engulfed
in all my strength, provided that for ever
my name remains upon the ocean depths!

# Sadness

Sadness, today you come down from the Sun.
Your changeable appearance is the gloomy
sky, and the sea in spumy
ripples the edges of your linen gown.

Alone like Ermione, so alike:
she comes in silence up to you alone,
trailing in winglike ripples her white skirt.
So similar that I might well mistake,
except that on her cheek, still damp with rain,
I see a single lock, dark violet.
So many roses that
piled in her lap the topmost prickles her:
her chin is jewelled with a garnet drop.
Like bearded faun close up
close up there gnaws and nibbles at the roses
a dirty capricorn with cloven hoof.

# The Sea-Hours

Which of the Hours
that you led on
alive that turned ash-pale
like ghosts
with the going of the sun
in evening sadness,
O Ermione,
which of the Sea-Hours
that had your face
your hands your dress
and your light movements
all of your gestures
and each grace that was yours,
O Ermione,
Which of the Maiden-Hours
who tamed with silence
alone the savage sea
as if they
had gathered it into their lap
like a surly child
to soothe its pain
by smiling,
O Ermione,
which of the Hours that were divine
with the occult joys
you gave them,
goes with you where you travel
beyond the limpid rivers,
beyond green hills,
beyond the azure mountains?

That Hour who gathers
on barren sand
black leaves
from the sacred oak,
O Ermione?
Leaves – creatures of the mountains
consumed by bitter salt,

188

which the wind seized
from crags and gave to the bitter wave
which troubles and tosses them
and then rejects.
That Hour who gazes at the far
lighthouse upon the bare
rock where the wave breaks,
O Ermione?

A sleepless eye that burns
and now already turns
across the deserted mirror
its indefatigable fires.
Or that Hour who inclines
thoughtfully her ear
towards the seashell
to listen to the roar
of the whorls
and hear in them the trumpet,
Triton's trumpet who calls
the lost Siren,
O Ermione,
and hears in them the sea which weeps
the lost Siren?

Which of the Hours,
which of the Sea-Hours,
with the occult joys
you gave them,
with the secret language
you taught them,
O Ermione,
goes with you on your journey
beyond the limpid rivers,
beyond green hills,
beyond the azure mountains,
O Ermione,
beyond the shining cottages,
beyond oak-groves,
beyond the glorious azure mountains?

# A goddess of the shore

Summer, lovely at your exordium
carrying gentle gold inside your mouth
just as the Arno to its silent mouth
takes with it on its way persuasive calm!

And yet more lovely now your time has come
to sink in skies of faded azure with
your elbow as you sink towards your death
upon a western cloud that turns to flame.

Ermione upon your russet bed
is burning grains of amber which exhale
the weeping of your pines and their regret.

I from your final loveliness have made
a dancing goddess whence my heart is full:
Undulna, halcyon wings upon her feet.

# *Undulna*

Four halcyon-wings are on my feet,
a pair upon each ankle-bone,
blue and green, and they guide my flight
curving erroneous on the brine.

My pale legs where the light shines through
are like the wandering jellyfish
in waves with the white pancrazio
and sea-kale in a shapeless mass.

I conduct the waves in perfect measure
and make them spread along this shore
alga, sea-lettuce make a bitter
tangle-entangled garland for.

I regulate the lines of foam
left shining at the water's edge:
from the oldest to the one just come
I arrange them in a fine collage.

Human musicians use various modes,
Doric to Phrygian, in their works:
infinite tunes for the endless gods
are what I make from the faintest of marks.

Notes of the waves are what I write
on the wet sand; I write and run,
and rapidly I alternate
the chords and pauses of a tune.

O sand, my sheet of melody,
not one of your tiniest grains of rock
would I give for the pumice hidden away
by the spring which the ilex makes so dark.

You shine, sand, in your countless grains
on my script that is shaped like the sickle moon;
while the water you drink makes you more dense,
and barren salt makes you more firm.

191

These signs are in a relief so low,
and traced with such care and sober art,
that even a child's arching brow
seems not so fine and delicate.

A three-furrowed track now and again
cuts right across the wavy line;
a human print, when it presses down,
is filled with light and seems to smile.

Such tracks in this jarring harmony
are the shapes of neumes, or very like.
O curving lyre on which I play
and no fingers nor plectra ever pluck!

I travel across like the wind; this great
concert is mine who make no sound
from the nails upon my silver feet
to where my forehead's lightly veined.

With an easy ear I can make out
the tones of the wave as it comes to me,
and clear-eyed I investigate
the slightest sign that is far away;

so that the musical traces are full
of sound for me where now today,
sensing the calm is panting still,
I read the storm of yesterday.

What is this whiteness like no other
which shines across the shores and spreads?
Thetis giving to Core's mother
salty wreaths for her mourning weeds?

Can it be that the calm of halcyon days,
before the winter, 's in the air
from Ionian archipelagos
up to the mouth of the Serchio here?

Mildest September, the Flute-player
moving through orchards of our land,
eyes violet like wistaria,
youthful of face, curls all around,

scatters his brightness far and wide,
sounding through two bones of a crane –
stretched in the shadow of the red
fruits of the arbutus – his tune.

The sea breathes gently like a child
held in his mother's lap and calm.
Halcyon days make the sea mild,
gold milk against the wintertime.

No wave gets up; there's not the slight-
est wash or ripple heard or seen.
The lucky shore enjoys the light
by the ocean of oblivion.

The sand is endlessly glitterful,
rejoicing in each smallest grain.
Such sparkle from the polished shell,
the dead medusa, the fish-bone.

No slightest sound's made anywhere
by the light, the silence beams in candour.
Well-marbled Pania raises her
stupendous rocks in all their splendour.

Between Magra and Serchio
the sea is charmed. There are not any
sails. O mid-autumn, I feel as though
I am about to taste your honey!

Already the scent of the new wine
comes from the dry vineyard like smoke.
And in the dawn the August moon
looked like a sickle worn with work.

Friend of this work, the Sun is moving
out from the Maiden to the Scales;
already the quarrels he is hurling
have fewer feathers in their tails.

A silence like that of death throughout
the sea and sky now both are clear!
Summer is passing away, stretched out
in the golden glory of her hair.

I pause. Summer is passing on.
No wave gets up. The expansive white
is still. I hear trembling low down
the halcyon wings upon my feet.

The shores are white and stretching, while
between water and sand the zone
on which I write with fleeting skill
disappears. I smile upon the calm.

Now at my feet the billow's mark,
burdened with black of scraps and tatters,
warps, a wet branch of a leafy oak
is lying between two little feathers,

and a dry fir-cone now opened wide,
which hung in a sounding pine once heavy,
lies by a round medusa spread
out and a single laurel-berry.

There butterflies like snowflakes come
trembling in couples and huge flights;
and in the light they look like foam
drifting about in loving rites.

Their shadows are azure on the sea
like scattered flowers of the aconite,
flickering so that it seems to me
the trembling expanse is infinite.

# The Thessalian

Among these boles, where roots are complicated
and poison fungus has begun to swell,
I hear a scarcely recognizable
uncloven heel clashing like bronze being battered.

It cannot be a wild horse: it has clattered
too steadily; too loud too long a while
through the wild wood this uncontrollable
unreachable kind of galloping has lasted.

Crushing where cones and rugged roots encumber,
these are the solid hooves of Thessaly,
the twofold Centaur safe and sound from battle.

He'd like to find himself, while young September
weaves rushes round the glass fragility,
drinking dark wine out of a swollen bottle.

# The goatskin

## I

The hide upon a dirty billy goat
I was, before knives came and cut me clear.
How stinking in the springtime of the year
he was among the she-goats, prone to butt,

believe me you who hear; with surly look,
bearded, and with hard wattles on his throat,
with rugged horns that never lost a fight,
with sulphur in his eyes, black as a rook!

He was lusty, and he had wives enough;
he could be savage when it came to it;
but like a satyr, when the rustic flute
was sounding, danced erect on cloven hoof.

Once slaughtered he was really on the hook
and dripping blood; he fumed ripped open: lights
and liver flaming red, and all his guts
quite obvious even to a casual look.

I was pulled wet and flabby from his back.
Iron scraped hair and shreds of carnage off.
And a good mixture for the tanning trough
came from vallonia and bitter bark.

Dried in dark cubicles, and ironed out
with boulders, and then stretched again to dry,
fate had me stitched and sewn up accurately:
my seamstress knew just how to manage it.

I was a goatskin, a fat prince of skins
at all the reservoirs and all the wells.
I was filled up from ditches and from rills,
from the eternal springs, and from the rains,

196

and with fresh water; but it had an odour
always and always had a taste of goat,
so that the women used to add a lot
of mint and aniseed to change the flavour.

The skin, O man, envies your raging thirst!
Dry scorching plains, and livid stony ground,
feverish coastal marsh, gravel and sand
which burn in dried-up rivers in the waste,

panting pack-animals, the creak of carts
I got to know, and the fixed gaze of thirst.
I was worth more than the whole universe
to desperate desire of parching throats!

O man, from kindly gods you have derived
your thirst. The poppy and the gillyflower
burn ardently, but never with such power
as all the thirsty mouths I satisfied.

Not he whence I was plundered, my own goat,
charged with such force as people used to do
to drink from me. I drenched them through and through.
Oh pleasure of the gurgle in the throat!

Now I am seized, my swollen sides are pressed
by griping hands (it seems to me dry eyes
drink before lips), in griping hands I rise
to faces that are burnt and white with dust.

From me each vein each artery is filled
with liquid joy, down even to the most
far places of the heart. Empty at last,
I feel I've quenched the thirst of all the world.

## II

A brother to the wrinkled bag they fill
with onions, crusts of bread, and all together,
I now became though empty. No more water
did I hear splashing in the ice-cold pail,

but from the swelling udder I could hear
inside the cattle-shed the milk pressed out.
So gods assigned to me a further fate,
to make my tedious life less of a bore.

Swollen with milk, I too looked like an udder,
but more capacious and less pink. At dead
of night I hung inside the cattle-shed,
like one less uberous beneath a mother.

But never was the goatskin such a friend
to peace as at the back end of the year
when it fulfilled the function of a jar
for oil as the chaste Pallas had designed.

The olive brings us peace, being slow and fat.
Once it has wailed and wept beneath the stone,
it grows more mild and never speaks again;
while water has a thousand tongues that chat.

And now Palladian chastity enough
filled me and silence. Speechlessly I heard
the grandmother's weak temples pulsing, bread
yeastily rising in the kneading-trough.

Then of a sudden, while I lay one night
up on the shelf with many a lesser jar,
there came along a shaggy fleece-clad boor
who took me to – I had no notion what.

On me his hand felt hard as stone, the claw
of some ferocious beast his curving nail.
The Bears were setting. At a horrible
wood, on a river-bank, he made a pause.

Face down in his own blood there lay stretched out
his enemy. He cut away the head
with a sharp sickle; that truncated head
he took by the hair, to load me with the weight.

198

All of a sudden I was full of sinful
black blood. The sickleman said to the skull:
'You're thirsty? Here's the chance to drink your fill
of undiluted liquor. Have a skinful.'

He sealed the skull he sealed the blood inside me.
They made me swell. And then he lifted me.
Onto the river's bank he shifted me.
Into the middle of the stream he shied me.

The liquor was still boiling up like mad.
Believe me, men who hear, spring water, white
milk, gentle oil, all I had had inside,
are nothing to the wonder of your blood!

Brief bloody war was waging; I was filled
with storm immeasurable and soon allayed.
I did not really feel it was a head,
but rather spinning in me all the World.

In fluvial chill that load changed into clots
of blood and bloody matter; and the stream
rolled me between its banks, and in its gloom
carried me rapidly to foreign parts.

### III

It was at daybreak in the willowtrees
the biform Satyr rediscovered me.
Your dozy spirit can no longer see,
O man, the old Italian deities!

They're still alive, and they are full of power:
they breathe the breath of woods and woodland spaces;
the mountain ridges are their holy places;
they still bear witness to themselves up there.

Mankind, you do not see them any more.
Your heart is breaking up like fruit gone bad.
Your mother Earth feeds you with all that's good
and all in vain. You weep in front of her!

199

The Satyr found me, and he was divine.
He chuckled deep within his tawny hide;
and then he stole away with me to hide
me in the trees: he thought me full of wine.

He licked his lips in his anticipation
while opening me. But did not turn a hair
at skull and clotted blood. 'What have we here?
Without a doubt the head of the great Thracian!'

On to the grass he shook my horrid weight,
then shook me. Then he gathered up the skull,
rolled it about, and hurled it with a yell
into the Serchio: 'Orpheus' head you're not!'

The laugh that rattled out through his rough teeth
was like a pebbly brook. And then in clean
water he washed me; dried me. Then again
he curved his lips to fill me with his breath.

Full of divine afflatus, I became
the spirit of the earth at its most wild!
And then the Faun arrived, one little skilled
at swimming in the pure and limpid stream.

The god his father gave him me; so that
up on the surface I supported him
in all the efforts that he made to swim
moving too fast his little cloven feet.

This kid had all a roebuck's whitish fur
down from the navel, but apart from that
his body was all smooth; his nose was flat;
his eyes were squint and rather sinister.

He used to keep me underneath his arm,
there where some scattered strands of reddish hair
were sprouting; and I lived in mortal fear
of being punctured by his little horn,

for he was quickly roused to childish anger,
striving to free his foot from water-weeds,
seeing the wild duck fly up from the reeds,
or feeling pikes flash by him in the water.

Green Serchio in low woods of weed and rush!
Mornings in summer, when this small blond Faun
covered in pink hibiscus flowers came down
with snares for ducks and wicker pots for fish!

Alas, his lessons went on swimmingly.
By now he knew to cleave the swiftest stream;
and more and more the goatskin lay alone
in mud, till it was empty finally.


IV

But the high gods were once more kind to me.
A pleasant shepherd with a golden beard
found me, and picked me up and, in the shade
thrown by a laurel, started work on me.

He made for me four little tubes of box
of different lengths, and then he smoothed them down.
In my shoulder he fixed the shortest one
and tied it there with string treated with wax.

In my mouthpiece he fixed the other three,
one longer, and the other two quite short,
and in the longer one he made a lot
of holes, that they might all sound diversely.

The shorter two, one narrow and one broad,
both opening out into a bell below,
were there to make the burden high or low
like wind-swept foliage to the singing bird.

A miracle! He breathed into the short
tube and he made the new-born bagpipes swell!
Then a young woman with her features full
of happiness came walking to the door,

her fine arms bare, and said: 'Look what is born,
O Goldenbeard, dear husband, just for us:
enormous riches in our little house;
see all the granaries fill up with grain,

see the hives filling with the work of bees,
the orchards fill with apples all of gold,
see Love's own roses – all the gardens filled,
see all the woodland full of stags and does;

and I shall have inside my pictured house
a marriage bed with four enormous pillars,
and dresses I shall have of many colours,
and every kind of wreath to wreathe my brows;

and I shall have and I shall have again
a thousand maids to spin my wool for me;
while all my sisters I shall give away
as brides to Asian satraps one by one!'

Such was the great enchantment that they made,
goatskin and shepherd, with a breath of air,
believe me you who hear, a breath of air,
and with divine Apollo's timely aid;

because the god who plays the lyre, the god
who stripped the wretched Marsyas of his skin,
is very generous with his divine
help to rough shepherd and to learned bard

with three-stringed tortoise-shell or hollow reed,
if but a candid heart is offered up.
Evenings and dawns like wandering flocks of sheep
we pasture in our rustic solitude.

The soft fig swelled upon the bristling pine,
narcissi bloomed upon the junipers,
the greyhound in his collar danced with hares,
and new was old and old was new again.

Wonder of wonders! As towards the Sun
the sunflower turns, so at that charming sound
the lady in the doorway stopped and turned.
The lintel breathed of the Athenian

Daedalus, and the rough jamb seemed a column
of Pelops' Palace with the ivory shoulder,
when but the shepherd sang: 'I love your pallor,
O lady, paler than the white alburnum!'

She had become more pale lapped in that sound,
as flax when soaked in water turns pure white.
Distaff and spindle – she just smiled and smiled –
shuttle and heald were left to lie around.

He seized her of a sudden by her hair
that was as black as grapes at harvesting,
as thick as hyacinths that bloom in spring,
as ivy-berry-clusters curling round.

He seized her of a sudden by her hair;
Death seized her, knocked her down, and through his gloom
he dragged her; way beyond the curving stream
Death bore her to the darkness of his land.

And no one no one saw her ever again.
Deep gloomy silence fell upon the farm.
The shadow fell across the door, and came
into the marriage bed. There was no dawn.

And no lament was heard inside the farm:
flintstone was there instead of heart and eyes.
The lizard fled away from off the tiles,
the swallow fled away, the bee was gone.

By the sad fireside I was hanging up.
And at the last the goatskin came to mind.
The silent shepherd gazed at me awhile.
He came, he took me, and he did not weep.

And then for one more time I seemed to be
pressed lightly by his forearm to his side,
and the obstruction of his grief was cleared
as he gave vent to all of it through me.

'Now let me follow in your steps, my wife!'
And then with cruel hand he tore out all
my pipes, and broke them. And his naked soul
and us he offered up to Stygian Night.


V

O you who listen, how unkind fate was
to me. For I was granted little rest
by the high gods. Winters and summers passed;
autumns and springs – the saffron and the rose.

All things recur; all wisdom is in vain.
Wisdom's not worth a fig, or fig-tree wood,
or goat-droppings. I would prefer, as a good
pupil of Liber, ending up insane.

Though corpulent, much have I seen and heard
as the friend of travellers who could not rest,
as connoisseur of many a different taste,
servant to all the world, to man and god.

I held so much, of what was pure, what mixed.
The true the false are the alternate leaves
upon one twig: there is no sage that lives
that can discern precisely which is which.

And, like wool, virtue can be dyed in grain,
and like Vertumnus our beatitude
changes its shape. I would prefer, as a good
pupil of Liber, ending up insane.

How different in their quality I've found
water, and milk, and smooth and silent oil,
and human blood and satyr's breath, as well
as all the metamorphoses of sound.

204

But that red liquid which can render you
like gods, O man, I have not known at all:
that which the Satyr thought had made me swell!
I hear his laughter ringing out anew.

O man, you picked me up inside the den
where the wolf cub had dragged me in his game.
What am I worth? You see what I've become!
Join me, and let us both end up insane.

I do not want adventures any more.
I do not want to live a longer life.
Sew up the shoulder where I had the pipes
of sounding box and tighten up my jaw.

With one who's old like me what can be done?
Well, for the satisfaction of your thirst
you owe a sort of offering to the Earth.
So pour new wine into the ancient skin!

You will with songs of joy harvest the grape.
You will ferment from gentle must strong wine.
And with its youthful vigour, when the moon
is scarcely nascent, you will fill me up,

to be split open by that youthful vigour!
Then cover me and crown me with wild flowers,
and on that leafiest laurel-branch of yours
suspend me. I shall cut a marvellous figure!

I shall crack open at the height of noon.
Thunder will echo through the blaze of day.
And you will speak, your forehead bent to pray:
'Drink what I offer, Earth. I am your son.'

# The signs

Alas, the vineyard is oppressed with languor
like a fine lady lying on a bed
of purple hangings, who awaits her lover.

Alas, the shrub glows crimson, clematis
is dry and almost ashen-coloured, softer
than the first down that blooms upon a goose.

Alas, some reeds already are distent,
down in the slime the cotton-grass is open,
the frog makes his habitual lament.

Alas, I've glimpsed at times a mauve grey bloom
which is most probably a meadow saffron,
and seen the chaffinch take a yellow tone.

A creature by the side of the canal!
There where among slow images of clouds
the sweet soft flesh of grass is getting stale.

He was shaggy. On him I fixed my gaze;
and then I saw the death of what I liked
within his squinting and black-speckled eyes.

# Dreams of distant places

## The shepherds

September, it's time we went. Time for migration.
Now shepherds in my land of the Abruzzi
forsake the folds and travel to the ocean
which is for them the savage Adriatic
as green as are the pastures on the mountains.

They have drunk deeply of the alpine fountains,
so that the taste of native water may
remain in exiled hearts and offer comfort
and long beguile their thirsts along the way.
They have renewed their hazel-staffs again.

Taking the ancient drovepath to the plain,
as if upon a silent grassy river,
they walk in footsteps of the ancient fathers.
Now hear his voice, the first to catch the shiver
and quiver of the coastal waves once more!

And now the flock are walking by the shore.
In changeless air without a breath of wind.
The sun is yellowing the living wool
until it scarcely differs from the sand.
A wash, a trample, noises that are precious.

And why, I ask, am I not with my shepherds?

## The baths

September, today I'd like to see the azure
disk your sky makes when filling out the round
mouth of the mask that is fashioned out of stone
up on the top of the column which is flaking
through centuries, enveloped by the rosebush
shedding its petals hourly, in the square
cloister that with its yellowish travertine
brightens the red brick of the ancient Baths.

Of Orpheus I would reason then perhaps
with Hermes on the fountain's edge where dolphins
support the basin with their tails erect;
or hear perhaps the grave admonishment
the two black cypresses which still survive
appear to give two small green cypresses
growing exactly where their elders fell
when stricken by the lightning of July.

Or else, perhaps, beyond the myrtle, I
would seem to hear the panting of the slave
yoked with the beast of burden to the bar
around the conic millstone out of lava;
and more than naked torsos, more than busts,
more even than the cippi I'd find precious
the shadows of the butterflies on vases
the peasant farmer leadenly restored.

September, there, upon the fine throne's side,
Aphrodite's, the flautist with the eyes
like almonds and the breasts as small as quinces
lies, one thigh crossed and laid upon the other,
stretched out and always blowing on her double
flute with the fragments of her practised fingers;
and the immobile Shepherd King in basalt
holds to Eternity his crumbling eyes.

And in the orchards, silent otherwise,
of the white monks, defunct, the bees are buzzing;
the gods that live inside the cells are pagan,
the Maenads always tear apart their victim,
Anaximander thinks, and from the wall
is heard the sequence of the Arval Brethren.
'Enos Lases iuvate.' A honey-bee
goes in where Julia's solid locks beguile.

It shuts itself inside a cell-like curl.

## The flock and the herd

September, were I by the Loricino
with you! It soothed the praetor in his trouble-
free times; it runs along on almost-rosy
sand rough with wrinkles and beflecked with sable,
the very look my greyhound's palate has.

The swallows fly above that fragile glass
delighting as they shatter it with white
breasts: a loose feather runs towards the sea.
And way beyond the emerald reeds the mountains
of Cori are celestial like the sea.

Vigour of Lazio, how you're dear to me!
Forgotten cities of the ancient kings,
halls where the imperial Lyrist liked to play,
a fine young lad is coming with his goats
and rules this coast, king of the Latin line!

His herd in its proportion is divine,
resembling in its blackness and its white
the wingèd flock that flies above the river,
an equal holocaust to Day and Night.
An opening flower the narrow estuary.

It smiles on goats and swallows equally.


## Lacus Iuturnae

September, clear and fresh and sweet are waters
where you may find your gentleness reflected;
and sweetly locked in memory my native
Aterno in its bed of bending grasses,
the Amaseno finally extinguished
with its Uffente where the Appian passes,
and the Cyane, reedy, well protected,
the Vella with its clematis vitalba.

209

And full of godhead from the hills of Alba
once more for me Diana's mirror shines.
But other water vivifies my dream.
This, till the urn is full, you draw for me.
Under the Palatine's pale reddish dome
near to the Temple of the Heavenly Twins
the Fountain of Iuturna is Rome's eye.
Oh for my love, mysterious at such distance!

High in the Forum in the noonday silence
stand the three columns out of Parian marble
as though they were of silver with salt-stains.
The black holm-oaks on the imperial hill
look like the primal woods in their remains.
The dull red basalt of the Sacred Way
glows in amongst the youthful oleanders
where ancient Latins sleep in their long home.

The Fountain, in its polished marble, 's dumb
as when Tarpeia, legendary Vestal,
descended to it with her earthen jar.
Maidenhair fern is quivering on the tuffa
and brick; the water, which is glaucous, tints
its marble bed; a lizard, undisturbed
on the Twins' altar, bathes in the warm air,
lapped by the goddess with the endless torch.

Butterfly shadows in that peace! And such
slight water drawn, sanctity of the City!
Do guardians of the everlasting Fire
go down still to the marble-guarded water?
Do Heavenly Twins, reddened with Latin slaughter,
go down to give to drink their steaming horses?
Oh for fresh laurels! Near the parapet
they're growing for me in Iuturna's shrine.

Where Hope is watching by them, taciturn.

## The loggia

September, how your little brother April
cast flowers upon the ruins of San Marco
at Capodistria, when we sailed our native
sea which Trieste with its moles like molars
holds in a love that's ever more emphatic.

Capodistria, cropped flower of the Adriatic!
I saw, in the loggia of a rustic palace,
house-martins' nests built on the blackened beams
among sorb-apples hanging in great bunches.
The weather ashen-coloured, damp and mild.

Along sea routes which leave no wake behind
you bring the flights of black and white together,
some from Pirano doubtless, some Parenzo,
and all of them united out at sea
with other parties coming from Chioggia.

The nests are now deserted in the loggia,
and of the bunches of sorb-apples only
the canes remain perhaps while slip-knots hold.
And such the way of speaking in the shadow
Rialto, Cannaregio come to mind.

A dove is moaning on the frieze outside.


## The pack

September, now upon the Lombard plain
the pack of bloodhounds is already ready,
a splendid pack, tawny and spotted bloodhounds
with ears as soft and white and palpable
as withered petals of magnolia blossom;
bloodhounds for hunting fox and fallow-deer,
already on the scent in thorn and heather,
with tails erect and tipped in shining white.

211

A lengthy bridge; Sesto Calende by it.
Ticino, through the shrubs and scattered thickets
you run towards a dam of rosy granite,
you foam and froth in regular descent,
like fleeting cloth upon the rapid loom,
a web with snowy blossom woven over.
The locks are closed by ancient artifice,
the work of Leonardo, godlike man.

Ticino, smile of the Lombardic plain,
you are the smile which lingers to his glory –
the craftsman who once held you in his hand –
and the compacted day of his close ladies.
Oh glades among the bushes where the gold
is turning red, glades gently warm and pleasant,
so like the laps of ladies that are longed-for
that trampling there's repugnant to the rider!

The hounds are running through the springy heather,
tails in the air and muzzles to the ground,
under the master of the hunt who trains them
for long pursuits to start in mid-October.
Their yelping is heard clearly through the silence,
and horns are heard recalling those that scatter
and those that pant behind lolling their tongues.
The best of them already show their mettle.

That master of his art is in fine fettle:
at times it almost seems the scented Summer
is breathing out its very last beneath
the horse's hooves curvetting as it gallops.
The training done, the master slows his steps
along the cart-track cluttered up with faggots,
taking his pack of hounds towards the kennel,
towards Oleggio rich in spinning-mills.

The moors grow misty as the stream exhales.

212

## The carobs

September, now the carobs have matured,
and now across the hot Cilician Sea
it's you who pilot from the shores of Cyprus
the saica, round of hull and square of sail.
Calm on the sea, and sapphire with no cloud.

The germa with four sails more huge than any
you also pilot to Sardinia,
the garbo, the schirazzo – Levantine
ships with their freight of grateful dark-brown beanpods.
And with you comes the sickening smell of honey.

The siliqua, on which the mules grow fat
and light of step, which takes in time of famine
their hunger from the peasants with white teeth,
is glowing as your chestnut hair is glowing
while you are on the crow's-nest looking out.

Yes, oil of sesame anoints your hair
arranged no doubt like ivy-berry-clusters.
Such sweetness on the sea that the forgotten
hymn once again, which once in Amatunte
rose to the Cyprian, rises in the air.

September, were we with you everywhere!

# New moon

New moon, September!
In the distant ether
the face of the creature
of heaven whose name
is Luna, translucent as
the medusa is,
or hoarfrost at dawn,
as fleeting as
snow on the water,
or foam on the sand,
as pale as
pleasure is
upon a pillow,
this pallid face is giving up,
growing more pale and languid,
with a carcanet
under her chin and so bright
as to darken it:
silent colourless face
of the creature
of heaven whose name is Luna,
under whose chin is a curving
carcanet so bright
as to darken it,
in that distant ether
her name was Diana
among her nymphs the stars,
her name was Selene
with the white arms
when she loved that young man
the shepherd Endymion
who slept in her white arms
for ever and ever.

New moon, September!
In the ambiguous light
of the day without flame
and the shadeless night,

214

the sea, more gentle
than the sky in its slow
rolling, more soft
than the cloud
of milk which the mount
expresses from out
of its delicate breasts,
the sea works to accompany
the melody
of the earth, the melody
the flutes of the crickets,
hardworking and hoarse,
make in the peace of the fields,
the melody
which the frogs
make in the dead
of the swamps where the river
stagnates in mud
between willow and reed,
the melody made
among osiers
and made among rushes
on distant banks
by lonely men
weaving baskets
out of young twigs,
holding again and again
the words of the refrain
returning ever.

New moon, September!
There is such clarity
in the light the day and night
are still pouring out
not sadly not happily
on the sea in its bed
that you can still see
the waves of the wind
on the sand, the tracks
of children, the empty

shells, the silver
seaweed,
the cuttlefish bones,
the pods
of the carobs,
you can see in the hedge
the bare berries
of the dog-rose redden
and the corn cob shine in the field
bearded with gold
which when the moon is full
on the threshing floor
will be winnowed with song,
and in the vineyard
the cluster of gold
which used to be loud with bees,
and in the garden the fig
which from its navel
oozes honey,
and on the threshold of the hovel
see the distaff whiten
as the ancient mother spins,
spins ever.

New moon, September,
gentle as the face
of the creature
of heaven whose name
is Ermione, and warm
as her hair,
moist as the smile
of her mouth
still moist
from the first ripe grapes and the must,
slight as her sash
in the sky which is green
like her dress!
She has shivered
in the green
of her dress which is fragrant

at every step,
like a shrub at every breath,
she has shivered
in the first chill of the night
who in the noonday went to sleep
with her cheek
on her curving arm
and awakened with her temples
damp, with her lip
pearled, in the warmth,
glowing red like a dawn
sprinkled with dew,
and smiling.
And I say: 'O Ermione,
you have been shivering.
Yes August too, yes August too
has gone away for ever!

Look at the sky of September.
In the distant ether
the face of the creature
of heaven whose name
is Luna, with a carcanet
under her chin so bright
as to darken it,
this pallid face gives up the ghost...'
But Ermione speaks,
neither joyful nor sad:
'You are wrong. What is bright
is the sickle
of Summer, the sickle
which Summer lets fall
as she dies, the sickle
which sickled the awns
and the poppy and cornflower
when they were blooming
to make me a coronal
brighter than sky or blood;
and it is the face of Summer
which fails and pales

in the distant ether, which dies
in its own brightness
on the waters,
between the day without flame
and the shadeless night,
after we loved it so much,
after we liked it so much;
and her song
of leaves of wings of breezes of shade
of scents of silences and of waters
stays mute for ever;

and the melody of September,
which is made by the rustic flute
to accompany
the sea in its slow lament,
is not heard up there in the distant
ether where she breathes out
in loneliness
her spirit with its scent
of seaweed of rosin of laurel;
and the man who lingers
as he weaves young twigs
once gathered the grain in sheaves
and now makes baskets
for grapes, to a sort of singsong,
and everything is forgotten;
August also will be
lost in the scent of the must,
in the sound of the golden bee;
oblivion everywhere,
oblivion everywhere;
and no one will know any more
how very pleasant could be
the shadows of flights
over salty sands,
the tracks of birds
in the rivers' clays
unless I do, unless I do,
unless she does who is going

away beyond clear rivers,
beyond green hills,
beyond the azure mountains,
unless she does who is going
who is going far off for ever,

and not like your swallows, September!'

# Envoi

Mount Mommio pours towards the jacinth sky
its olive trees, a sort of pallid veil,
as on some island in the Ionian Sea
a Grecian hill.

And Monte Magno in a rather dull
silver has swathed its massive pyramid;
Matanna purples like the flexible
flower of the reed.

By Camaiore's streams the reeds are loud:
I know by heart the song they're making for me.
Could I but see the arbutus glow red
upon Mount Darme!

Standing upon viburnum-rich Cape Crow,
Palmaria with its pines could I but see,
that clothed in mourning of black marble-stone
lies solitary!

Oh could I only hold you in my hand,
as though a vase from an Etruscan tomb,
region of Luni, with your marble and
your butcher's-broom,

your aromatic woods, their sandy floors,
your hard Promethean materials,
the eagle round your peaks, the floating flowers
on your canals.

Oh could I with my art, from Val di Serchio
to Val di Magra and to the Vara too
and to the Gulf, hold you within a circle
as your Alps do!

Too heavy on my heart lies my departure.
As though it left its body, from the white
marble between Versilia and Carrara
my soul takes flight.

A time to die. In water that is dead
the sweet soft flesh of grass is getting stale.
There is, though sound of sickle is not heard,
a deathly smell.

The ruins of Ceràgiola glow red,
where the Versilia from two streams is filled,
as if from every splinter cruel blood
ran and congealed.

Gàbberi like a metal basinet
rises in rough and rocky nudity.
And look, on highways over there they cart
the sedge away.

Great sickles cut it in Quiesa's shade
where Massaciùccoli gets swampy, where
young shoots ray from the willow like a head
of flaming hair,

in little reeds that rustle turning gold,
in slow esparto grass of pallid brown.
The kingfisher, a flash of emerald,
goes streaking down.

Oh were I on a barge, moving to stem
the floating weeds, with reed-mace and sparganium
my heavy load, with fixed upon the stem
a huge bucranium

or a red kite with spreading wings, and where
a scent of pinks was rising from the heap
from certain rushes with red roots piled there,
while all the sap

so precious to the working perfumer
dripped from the herbs; and could I only lie
upon my back and stare at and admire
the jacinth sky;

caught between sky and water, could I follow
along its course the Fossa Burlamacca,
where like the fields of asphodel the hollow
is growing whiter,

the bargee meanwhile hauling on his rope
along a songless bank; while I, at ease
on heaped-up herbs, seem safe upon the slope
that leads to Dis!

But evening falls, the time comes I must go,
who feed my heart on dreams and fruitlessly.
Men take on heavy carts along white roads
the sedge away.

The overhanging heaps are piled so wide
that under them the poles just disappear;
they hide the yoke they hide the horns they hide
the labouring steer,

so that from far they seem to be self-moved;
each one makes up a monstrous animal
which, so deep is the dust, seems to be clothed
in thickest wool.

They move to Pietrasanta in a line
with their huge loads of stable-straw and dung.
One waggoner is bawling comments while
one sings a song.

And all Versilia takes a golden hue
with which the heart is torn. You never were,
Pania, as beautiful as you are now
in this last hour!

O Tyrrhene Sea, O Lower Sea, the Lighthouse
kindles its sleepless eye upon your mirror;
and you are guarded also by tremendous
steel ships, watched over

222

out of La Spezia, just behind Cape Crow
which is defensive for all Italy;
a splinter from Orion's sword the new
moon seems to be;

as soon as you are covered with night's shade,
the Pleiades will pour on you their tears
and over you the lazy Herd will lead
his starry Bears;

along the curving shores, but for your breath,
in changeless air and shade there is no sound;
you only mirror the enormous breadth
of sky around.

When I am far from here, O Alp, O Sea,
with my heart shrouded in a troubled cloud,
the peak my heart aspires to may be seen
in this clear ode!


Ode, once at last before I am exiled,
go up the Serchio, climb the hill again
to there where Virgil's last and greatest child,
his godlike son,

he who has studied and can comprehend
the hawk's call clashing and the dove's low moan,
who opens to the flower his childlike mind
and to the tomb,

he who has dared to look so very hard
into the blue and black eye that belong
to Alexander, and has even heard
Sappho's new song,

is sitting by a cypress silently
and not expecting you at all. Fly then!
No one will help to bring you on your way;
go all alone;

and he will welcome you with open hand,
though rapt in heald or bee or the deep chime
coming from Barga – many sorts of sound –
or his own rhyme.

Perhaps he has the book upon his knee
written by his own father (does he gather
the trefoil with the gift of prophecy,
the four-leafed clover,

to make a bookmark in the uncut pages
where Tityrus sings? or where Aeneas takes
such careful note of what the Sibyl rages
out of her rocks?).

Abandoning her needles – it is late –
perhaps his sister, smoothing back her hair,
and locking up her linen with its scent
of lavender,

goes to sit with him, sick at heart to see
swallows already gathering in the eaves.
'Accept, O son of Virgil' you must say
'these laurel leaves.

Accept them from your most affectionate friend.
To you he sends me now he must depart.
He's woven me (a garland for your head)
with all his art.

And who today will crown the learned bard
if not the bard the prince of loneliness?
See stupid Scythian and see painted Mede
praised among us;

and when barbarity coupled with wind
makes novel monsters for us, not again
does Phoebus with his silver bow descend
to strike them down.

But you preserve the very finest things,
my Host. And with a pulse that does not falter
old noble blood through your imaginings
runs strong as ever.

Your thought is strong to illuminate and feed
mankind, like tranquil olives putting out
Palladian berries which provide men food
and also light.

And so receive this garland from your brother
which I am bringing you: it has no weight:
its leaves are laurel leaves which last for ever
yet are so light.

Made from a slender bending branch that grew
where the Cor cordium had his funeral pyre
near Alp and Sea, and Buonarroti knew
artistic fire.

The craftsman as he made for you this crown
could see on shining Sagro the old wounds
and on Altissimo that peplos blown
back by the winds.

Another Mountain is that viewless one
he climbs while you climb the opposing slope.
One rage, though you are separate and alone,
urges you both.

Where have these bold hearts promised they will come
together on a day, but on the peak?
That day you will sing out one selfsame hymn
upon the peak.'

Speak to him in those very words, my Ode.
And, having done that, to his sister give
this lily known as the pancrazio,
the last I have.

# Glossary

*Abruzzi, my land of the*   D'Annunzio's native region of Italy. 'Dreams of distant places'.

*Achaea*   A region on the Gulf of Corinth; also Greece as a whole. 'Summer madrigals'.

*Achelous*   The name of several Greek rivers; d'Annunzio refers to the one which runs through Aetolia and Acarnania. 'Mouth of the Serchio'.

*Acheron*   A river in Hades. 'Second dithyramb'.

*Achradina*   A plateau, part of the city of Syracuse. 'The oleander'.

*Acqua Marcia*   The water, very cold and sparkling, of the Marcia aqueduct, which was over sixty miles long. 'First dithyramb'.

*Acroceraunian*   Of the mountain spurs in Epirus. Acroceraunia means 'Headlands of thunder'. 'Orphic anniversary'.

*Adriatic*   This sea, to the east of Italy, has long been proverbial for its storms. 'Dreams of distant places'.

*Aegean (Sea)*   The sea into which the River Hebrus flows. 'The youngster', 'Orphic anniversary'.

*Aegina*   A bay, and also an island on which there was a temple to Aphrodite to whom the dove was sacred. 'The youngster', 'Summer madrigals'.

*Aeneas*   In the sixth book of *The Aeneid*, Aeneas hears the prophecies which the Sibyl in her cave makes about him. 'Envoi'.

*Aeneas' nurse*   Caieta, nurse of Aeneas, gave her name to the Gulf of Gaeta near which she was buried ('Aeneid', VII, 1-2). 'First dithyramb'.

*Aethon*   One of the horses which pulled the chariot of the sun. 'Fourth dithyramb'.

*Affrico*   A tributary of the Arno, it runs between Fiesole and Florence. 'The youngster', 'By the side of the Affrico on an evening in June after rain'.

227

*Aglaia*   A Grace, her name means 'beauty'. 'The oleander'.

*Agrigento*   A town on the south coast of Sicily. 'The many-headed song'.

*Agrio*   Ardi's horse, its Greek name means 'wild, savage'. 'Mouth of the Serchio'.

*Agro, plain of*   The Agro Romano is the large plain in Lazio crossed by the Tiber. 'First dithyramb'.

*Alba, hills of / Alban Hills*   South-east of Rome. 'First dithyramb', 'Dreams of distant places'.

*Alberese*   A town at the foot of the Uccellina hill near the western shore of Italy. 'The asphodel'.

*Alcỳone*   Alcyone and Ceyx were so proud of their happy marriage that the gods punished them by changing them into birds, a halcyon (a species of kingfisher) and a diver respectively. The halcyon nested on or near the sea, and Zeus commanded that there should be a period of calm, usually said to be around the winter solstice, for her to hatch her eggs. 'Calm'.

*Alexander*   Alexander the Great. In his poem 'Alexandros' Giovanni Pascoli (1855-1912) speaks of Alexander's black eye as a symbol of hope and his blue eye as a symbol of desire. 'Roman sarcophagus', 'Envoi'.

*Altissimo, (Mount)*   In the Apuan Alps. 'The rupestrian peplos', 'Envoi'.

*Altivs egit iter*   'He soared upwards.' 'Altivs egit iter'.

*Amaseno*   A watercourse which runs into the Pontine Marshes. 'Dreams of distant places'.

*Amatunte*   A city on the south coast of Cyprus. 'Dreams of distant places'.

*Ambra*   Lorenzo de' Medici's poem 'Ambra' tells of the love of the god of the River Ombrone for the nymph Ambra. 'The youngster', 'The tributaries'.

*Amnisus*   A port of Knossos. 'Fourth dithyramb'.

*Amorgo*   An island in the Sporades, famous for its fine linen. 'The coronal of Glauco'.

*Anaximander*   Anaximander of Meletus, a Greek scientist and philosopher of the sixth century BC, seen here on a relief in the Baths of Diocletian. 'Dreams of distant places'.

*Androgeos*   The son of Pasiphae and Minos, killed in Athens by order of King Aegeus: the Athenians were jealous of his success in the Panathenaea. 'Fourth dithyramb'.

*Anthèdon*   A Boeotian city. 'Second dithyramb'.

*Antigone*   A daughter of Oedipus and Jocasta. When she performed the funeral rites for her brother, an act which had been forbidden by King Creon of Athens, she was put to death. In his 'Oedipus at Colonus' Sophocles has her speaking of the nightingales in the grove of Colonus. 'The youngster', 'Orphic anniversary'.

*Anxur*   The old name of Terracina, on the coast of Lazio, originally built at the top of a hill. 'First dithyramb'.

*Anzio*   A town on the coast of Lazio, once a refuge for pirates. 'First dithyramb'.

*Aonia*   The old name for Boeotia. 'Ocean laurel'.

*Aonian mount*   Mount Helicon, sacred to the Muses. 'The bard without a lyre'.

*Apheliotes*   The east wind. 'Fourth dithyramb'.

*Aphrodite*   The goddess of love. The Ludovisi Throne in the Baths of Diocletian has a relief of the birth of Aphrodite from the sea. 'Fourth dithyramb', 'Dreams of distant places'.

*Apollo (Phoebus)*   The god of the sun, of music and poetry, and of prophecy. He lusted for Daphne, she fled him, and in answer to her prayer for escape she was changed into a laurel. In 'The oleander' d'Annunzio retells the story, substituting the oleander for the laurel. 'First dithyramb', 'Second dithyramb', 'The oleander', 'Ocean laurel', 'The rupestrian peplos', 'The goatskin', 'Envoi'.

*Apollonian wings*   Of Apollo, as god of the sun. 'First dithyramb'.

*Apollo's white-haired augur*   Aruns, an Etruscan (Dante, 'Inferno', XX, 46-51). 'The rupestrian peplos'.

*Appian (Way)*   Begun in 312 BC, this road went south-east from Rome to Terracina (Anxur), and thence to Capua, and was later extended to Beneventum and Brundisium. 'First dithyramb', 'Dreams of distant places'.

*Apuan (Alps)*   Near the western coast of Italy, north of Pisa. 'Noon', 'Orphic anniversary', 'The coronal of Glauco'.

*Ardea, Danaean*   The city of Turnus, King of the Rutuli, it was founded according to legend by Danae ('Aeneid', VII, 408-413). 'First dithyramb'.

*Ardi*   A character invented by d'Annunzio, possibly inspired by one of his sons. 'Mouth of the Serchio', 'The prisoner', 'The wing on the sea'.

*Arethuse / Aretusa*   An Arcadian nymph after whom the god of the River Alpheus lusted. She fled from him and became a fountain in Ortygia, the island in Syracuse harbour; but Alpheus flowed under the sea and was united with the fountain. This myth is often connected with pastoral poetry, which originated in Sicily and sings of Arcadia, and this is why d'Annunzio addresses Arethuse in 'The hippocampus' as a 'Muse'. The 'rapacious Aretusa' of 'The wave' and the thieving nymph of 'The hippocampus' may have been suggested by a nymph of the same name who was one of the Hesperides, the guardians of a tree which produced golden apples. Aretusa in 'The oleander' ('that Aretusa who was Florentine') is a mortal woman but with attributes of the fountain/nymph. Any uncertainty in these poems as to whether she is a mortal or not is deliberate and characteristic of d'Annunzio's mingling of the human and the divine. 'Orphic anniversary', 'The oleander', 'The hippocampus', 'The wave'.

*Argentaro*   A large promontory on the Tuscan coast near Orbetello. 'The asphodel', 'Summer madrigals'.

*Argo*   The ship on which heroes sailed to recover the golden fleece. 'Second dithyramb'.

*Argolis*   A plain in Greece. 'The name'.

*Aricia*   D'Annunzio uses the Latin form of the name. Ariccia, as it is in modern Italian, is a town a few miles south-east of Rome, near where the sacred grove of Nemi was. 'First dithyramb'.

*Arno*  The river which rises in Falterona and runs through Florence and Pisa. 'The youngster', 'Beatitude', 'Peace', 'The tenzon', 'Mouth of the Arno', 'Between two Arnos', 'The tributaries', 'The camels', 'Orphic anniversary', 'Mouth of the Serchio', 'A goddess of the shore'.

*Arval Brethren*  Twelve priests charged in ancient times with the ceremony to propitiate the gods of agriculture – Mars and the Lares. The text of an Arval hymn (beginning 'Enos lases iuvate') survives on some fragmentary marble in the Baths of Diocletian. 'Dreams of distant places'.

*Asphodel*  A plant of the lily family, it was regarded by the ancients, probably because of the pallor of its flowers, as sacred to the dead, and it was said to flourish in Hades. 'The truce', 'The olive', 'The roots of song', 'Second dithyramb', 'The asphodel', 'Envoi'.

*Astioche*  A daughter of Niobe. 'Gombo'.

*Aterno*  The River Pescara, on whose banks d'Annunzio was born, was known in ancient times as the Aternum. 'Mouth of the Serchio', 'Dreams of distant places'.

*Athene*  See Pallas (Athene). 'The youngster'.

*Atrium*  A hall or palace. 'Mouth of the Serchio'.

*Attic*  Grecian. 'The asphodel'.

*Attica*  The region of Greece which includes Athens. 'The youngster'.

*Ausonia*  An ancient and literary name for Italy. 'Ocean laurel'.

*Author of the wooden cow*  Daedalus. 'The wing on the sea'.

*Avernus*  The underworld, Dis, Hades. 'Terra, vale!'.

*Awns*  The beards of barley, oats, etc. 'New moon'.

*Baccha*  D'Annunzio has given the name to a Bacchante. 'The coronal of Glauco'.

*Bacchante(s)*  The Bacchantes were worshippers of Bacchus, or Dionysus, the god of wine, given to frenzied revels. 'First dithyramb', 'Second dithyramb', 'Third dithyramb'.

*Bacchic*   Of Bacchus, frenzied, orgiastic. 'Orphic anniversary', 'The death of the stag', 'Fourth dithyramb'.

*Bacchylides*   A Greek lyric poet of the fifth century BC who celebrated in three odes King Hieron I of Syracuse. 'The oleander'.

*Balausta*   The fruit of the pomegranate. 'Ocean laurel'.

*Ballatetta*   An old Italian lyric form linked with music and dancing. 'Peace'.

*Barb*   Used as the name of a fish. 'The coronal of Glauco'.

*Barga*   Near the home of Giovanni Pascoli (1855-1912) whose poem 'L'ora di Barga' (Time at Barga) is concerned with the hour striking from that village. 'Envoi'.

*Basinet*   A helmet, more or less hemispherical. 'Envoi'.

*Baths*   The Baths of Diocletian in Rome, with the monumental remains and archaeological finds in their Museum. 'Dreams of distant places'.

*Bear(s)*   The constellations of the Great Bear and of the Little Bear or Cynosure. 'The oleander', 'The goatskin', 'Envoi'.

*Beatrice*   The beloved of Dante. 'Beatitude'.

*Berenice*   The name (pronounced with four syllables) was chosen by d'Annunzio for its general literary and mythological associations, e.g. with Coma Berenices (Berenice's Hair), rather than for any precise significance. 'The oleander'.

*Bifid*   Cleft in two. 'The youngster'.

*Bisenzio*   A tributary of the Arno. 'The tributaries'.

*Boeotian*   Of Boeotia in Greece, where Mount Helicon is. 'August festival'.

*Boötes*   A constellation beside the Great Bear. The meaning of the Greek is literally 'ox-driver'. See also Herd. 'The oleander'.

*Bucranium*   An ox-skull used as an ornament. 'Envoi'.

*Buonarroti*   More commonly known as Michelangelo. 'The mothers', 'Envoi'.

*Buti*   An area in the region of Pisa, famous for the fineness of its olive oil. 'August festival'.

*Càbiri* Mysterious divinities whose main shrine was in Samo-thrace. 'The Victory of Samothrace'.

*Caecuban* A wine of Lazio, famous in antiquity. 'First dithyramb'.

*Calci* An area in the region of Pisa, close to Buti, and rich in olives. 'August festival'.

*Camaiore* A town near the west coast of Italy, north of Pisa. 'August festival', 'Envoi'.

*Camerata* A hill between Florence and Fiesole. It was in a villa on Camerata that the storytellers of the 'Decameron' took refuge. 'The youngster'.

*Campania, promised* A region of Italy, forming a crescent along the Bay of Naples. It is described as 'promised' because of its fertility, as it were a promised land. 'First dithyramb'.

*Candid / candour* White / whiteness. 'The youngster', 'The ear of corn', 'Works and days', 'First dithyramb', 'The name', 'The mothers', 'The highest Alps', 'The oleander', 'Third dithyramb', 'The Victory of Samothrace', 'Fourth dithyramb'.

*Cannaregio* A district of Venice. 'Dreams of distant places'.

*Cape Crow* Capo Corvo, a promontory on the Gulf of La Spezia, near the mouth of the River Magra. 'Noon', 'August festival', 'Envoi'.

*Cape Plemmirio* Near Syracuse. 'The oleander'.

*Capodistria* A town, now called Koper, south of Trieste on the coast of Istria. Before World War One, Istria was Austrian; after that war it passed to Italy; after World War Two it became part of Yugoslavia. D'Annunzio calls Capodistria a 'cropped flower' because he believes it has been separated from its mother country, Italy, like a flower cut from its stem. 'Dreams of distant places'.

*Capraia* With Gorgona, an island which Dante implored to move to block up the mouth of the Arno in order to drown the inhab-itants of Pisa and so avenge the death of Ugolino ('Inferno', XXXIII, 82-84). 'Noon'.

*Capricorn* A goat. 'Fourth dithyramb', 'Sadness'.

233

*Carrara*   A town in the Apuan Alps, famous for its white marble. 'The mothers', 'Envoi'.

*Casentino*   A valley north of Arezzo, through which the Arno runs. 'The tributaries'.

*Cataphract*   A soldier in full armour. 'The wave'.

*Catenaia*   A mountain in the Casentino district. 'The asphodel'.

*Cèceri, Monte*   A hill between Fiesole and Settignano. 'Works and days'.

*Celio*   One of the hills of Rome. 'First dithyramb'.

*Centaur*   Centaurs were mythical creatures, half man and half horse, inhabiting Thessaly. They were said to spring from the union of Ixion with a cloud. 'The truce', 'First dithyramb', 'The coronal of Glauco', 'The death of the stag', 'The Thessalian'.

*Ceos*   An island of the Cyclades, the home of the poet Bacchylides, the nightingale of Ceos. 'The oleander'.

*Ceràgiola*   A mountain in the Apuan Alps, much excavated for its marble. 'The rupestrian peplos', 'Envoi'.

*Cerastes*   Horned snakes. 'The youngster'.

*Cèrato*   A river in Crete near Knossos. 'Fourth dithyramb'.

*Ceres*   The goddess of corn, Demeter. 'First dithyramb'.

*Chimera*   A mythical beast, with the head of a lion, the body of a goat, and the tail of a dragon, and breathing fire. 'The truce'.

*Chioggia*   A town on the Venetian coast. 'Dreams of distant places'.

*Chios, wine of*   The wine from Chios, an island in the Aegean, was famous in antiquity. 'The coronal of Glauco'.

*Chlamys*   A short cloak worn by horsemen in ancient Greece. 'The youngster', 'Mouth of the Serchio'.

*Choir*   The choir of the Muses on Helicon. See Muse. 'The hippocampus'.

*Chronos, son of*   Zeus, king of the gods. 'Fourth dithyramb'.

*Cilician Sea*   Between Cyprus and the coast of south-east Asia Minor. 'Dreams of distant places'.

234

*Cimino*   A mountain south-east of Viterbo in Lazio. 'First dithyramb'.

*Cippi*   A cippus is a monumental pillar. 'Dreams of distant places'.

*Circe*   A witch, the daughter of the Sun and Perseis, who lived on Circèo. 'First dithyramb', 'Mouth of the Serchio', 'Summer madrigals'.

*Circean*   Of Circe. 'Summer madrigals'.

*Circèo, Monte*   A rocky promontory, at one time an island, near Terracina (Anxur) in Lazio, the home of Circe. 'First dithyramb'.

*Cisa*   A mountain and a pass. 'The asphodel'.

*Cithaeron*   A Boeotian mountain where the Bacchantes held their revels. 'Fourth dithyramb'.

*City, burning*   Rome, burning with thirst. 'First dithyramb'.

*City, the*   Florence. 'Beatitude'.

*Cleossa*   A daughter of Niobe. 'Gombo'.

*Clio*   The Muse of history. 'The oleander'.

*Cloud*   Nephele, the mother of the Centaur by Ixion. 'Mouth of the Serchio', 'The death of the stag'.

*Colonus*   A grove of olives outside Athens. 'The youngster', 'Fourth dithyramb'.

*Colubers*   Snakes. 'The youngster', 'Fourth dithyramb'.

*Consecrate*   Consecrated. 'Fourth dithyramb'.

*Cor cordium*   The Latin phrase ('Heart of hearts') refers to Shelley on whose tomb in the English Cemetery in Rome it is inscribed. 'The asphodel', 'Envoi'.

*Core*   Proserpina, the daughter of Ceres / Demeter, who had to spend each winter in Hades, which is why her mother is said to need 'mourning weeds' in the autumn. 'Undulna'.

*Cori*   A town in Lazio. 'Dreams of distant places'.

*Corinth*   A city in the centre of Greece at the Peloponnesian end of the narrow isthmus which links the Peloponnesus to the mainland. 'Summer madrigals'.

*Corinthian bronze*   The bronze of Corinth, an alloy of gold silver and copper, was famous in antiquity. 'The death of the stag'.

*Corniglia*   A town of the Five Regions, famous for its wine. 'August festival'.

*Cornucopia*   The horn of plenty, the horn of the goat that suckled Zeus, the symbol of abundance and prosperity. 'The youngster', 'First dithyramb'.

*Corybantes*   The priests of Cybele whose rites involved loud music and wild dancing. 'Fourth dithyramb'.

*Cothurns*   Buskins, high boots worn in ancient times by actors in tragedy. 'Fourth dithyramb'.

*Cretan*   Of Crete. 'Fourth dithyramb'.

*Crete*   Large Greek island, one of whose most important towns in ancient times was Knossos. 'Fourth dithyramb'.

*Creusa's widower*   Aeneas. 'First dithyramb'.

*Curetes*   Ancient inhabitants of Crete, who celebrated a noisy worship of Zeus, like that of Cybele by the Corybantes. 'Fourth dithyramb'.

*Cyane*   A water-nymph of Syracuse, who protested at the abduction of Proserpina by Hades. Hades in his anger changed her into a spring of a deep blue colour. 'The oleander', 'Dreams of distant places'.

*Cybele*   The Great Mother, a personification of nature's fecundity. 'First dithyramb'.

*Cyclades*   An archipelago in the Aegean Sea. 'The coronal of Glauco'.

*Cynosure*   The Little Bear, the constellation which contains the North Star; also the North Star itself. 'The oleander'.

*Cyprian*   Aphrodite, whose cult was centred on Cyprus. 'Dreams of distant places'.

*Cyprus*   To the south of Asia Minor, a large island from whose waters Aphrodite was said to have been born. 'Dreams of distant places'.

236

*Daedalian*   Of Daedalus. 'Fourth dithyramb'.

*Daedalus*   A versatile artist and artisan. An Athenian by birth, he did his most famous work on Crete. He made the wooden cow in which Pasiphae consummated her love for a bull. The offspring of that union, the Minotaur, was kept in a labyrinth devised by Daedalus. He made wings for himself and his son Icarus. 'The wing on the sea', 'Fourth dithyramb', 'The goatskin'.

*Daemon*   Like Despot, Emperor, Lord, and Master, the poet's own genius, the inner voice whose commands must be obeyed. 'Altivs egit iter'.

*Danaean*   Of Danae. See Ardea. 'First dithyramb'.

*Dante*   Dante Alighieri, citizen of Florence, celebrant of Beatrice, author of the poem ('Donne ch'avete intelletto d'amore', from 'La vita nuova', XIX) quoted twice in 'Beatitude'. See Capraia and Gorgona. 'Beatitude', 'Noon', 'Orphic anniversary'.

*Daphne*   A Greek nymph, daughter of the god of the River Peneios. See Apollo. 'The oleander'.

*Darme, Mount*   In the Apuan Alps. 'Envoi'.

*Daughter of the Sun*   Pasiphae, daughter of the Sun and Perseis, and the wife of Minos of Crete. 'Fourth dithyramb'.

*Delos*   The island at the centre of the Cyclades. According to legend, it used to move about. 'Fourth dithyramb'.

*Delphic games*   They used to be held every four years at Delphi with participants from all over Greece. 'The many-headed song'.

*Delta, great*   That of the Nile. 'Mouth of the Serchio'.

*Demeter*   The goddess of corn, Ceres, mother of Proserpina. See Core. 'The youngster', 'The oleander', 'Third dithyramb', 'The asphodel'.

*Demogorgon*   A terrible deity, a character in Shelley's 'Prometheus unbound'. 'Orphic anniversary'.

*Dentex*   A fish. 'August festival'.

*Derbe*   A character invented by d'Annunzio. 'The oleander', 'The stag', 'The death of the stag', 'The asphodel'.

*Despot*   Like Daemon, Emperor, Lord, and Master, the poet's own genius, the inner voice whose commands must be obeyed. 'The truce'.

*Diana*   The goddess of hunting and chastity, sometimes identified with the moon. 'Versilia', 'New moon'.

*Diana's mirror*   The lake of Nemi, outside Rome, on the shores of which stood a grove sacred to Diana. 'Dreams of distant places'.

*Dicte*   A Cretan mountain sacred to Zeus who as a baby was protected there by the Corybantes, who covered his crying with their noise. 'Fourth dithyramb'.

*Diolkos*   The causeway made for hauling boats across the Isthmus of Corinth. 'The oleander'.

*Dionysus*   The god of wine. See Bacchante(s). 'First dithyramb', 'Second dithyramb'.

*Dis*   The underworld, Avernus, Hades. 'First dithyramb', 'Envoi'.

*Distent*   Distended, opened out. 'The signs'.

*Donatello*   The sculptor (1400-1482) whose 'white cathedral choirs' are preserved in the museum of the cathedral in Florence. 'The youngster', 'Mouth of the Arno'.

*Doric*   Of the region of Doris in Greece. Doric architecture was distinguished for its simplicity and massive strength. Doric music was stirring, solemn, simple, and martial. 'The youngster', 'The oleander', 'Undulna'.


*Eagle out of Thebes*   The Greek poet Pindar of the fifth century BC, born in Thebes. 'The oleander'.

*Earthshaker*   Poseidon, the god of the sea, causer of earthquakes. 'Fourth dithyramb'.

*Eleusis*   To the west of Athens, one of the most sacred sites in Greece. 'The youngster'.

*Elsa*   A tributary of the Arno. 'The tributaries'.

*Emmets*   Ants. 'Works and days'.

238

*Emperor* Like Daemon, Despot, Lord, and Master, the poet's own genius, the inner voice whose commands must be obeyed. 'The truce'.

*Emperor, merciless* Both Nero and Caligula came from Anzio. 'First dithyramb'.

*Endymion* A shepherd with whom Selene, the moon, fell in love. He was given perpetual sleep, and Selene descended nightly to embrace him. 'New moon'.

*Enos Lases iuvate* The beginning of a hymn of the Arval Brethren, one of the earliest pieces of literature in Latin, from fragmentary marble in the Baths of Diocletian. The meaning is probably 'O help us, ye Lares!' 'Dreams of distant places'.

*Eos* One of the horses which pulled the chariot of the sun. 'Fourth dithyramb'.

*Era* A tributary of the Arno. 'The tributaries'.

*Eracleos* A port of Knossos. 'Fourth dithyramb'.

*Erechtheum* On the Athenian acropolis, the temple of Athene and Poseidon. 'The youngster'.

*Eridanus* The River Po. 'Mouth of the Serchio'.

*Erigone* The name was chosen by d'Annunzio for its general literary and mythological associations, rather than for any precise significance. 'The oleander'.

*Erinys* One of the Furies. 'Third dithyramb'.

*Ermione* So called because of the associations mentioned in 'The name', Ermione is probably to be understood as the poet's usual companion in these poems even when, as for example in 'Between two Arnos' or 'Orphic anniversary', she is not named. Her original is Eleanora Duse but, as so often in d'Annunzio, the biographical and the fictional are deliberately fused. 'The rain in the pine wood', 'The name', 'Calm', 'The highest Alps', 'Sadness', 'The Sea-Hours', 'A goddess of the shore', 'New moon'.

*Etruscan (Sea)* Of the early, pre-Roman, inhabitants of Tuscany or Etruria. The Etruscan Sea is the Tyrrhenian or Lower Sea.

'The camels', 'Noon', 'The mothers', 'Orphic anniversary', 'The coronal of Glauco', 'Envoi'.

*Euryala*   A Gorgon, sister of Medusa. 'The many-headed song'.

*Evangelist*   Michelangelo's statue of Saint Matthew is a figure struggling as though trying desperately to free itself from the block of marble to which it is attached. 'The mothers'.

*Exhaust*   Exhausted. 'Fourth dithyramb'.

*Exordium*   The introductory part of a discourse or composition. 'A goddess of the shore'.


*Fabulist, ancient elegant*   Agnolo Firenzuola (1493-1543), author of 'Dialogo delle bellezze delle donne' (On the beauty of women). 'The tributaries'.

*Falterona*   The mountain where the Arno rises. 'Mouth of the Arno', 'The tributaries'.

*Faun(s)*   These ancient rural deities – represented as men with the horns tails and legs of goats – usually symbolized a happy sensuality. 'The truce', 'The youngster', 'Versilia', 'Sadness', 'The goatskin'.

*Faunus*   The Roman equivalent of Pan. 'First dithyramb'.

*Favonius*   The west wind, blowing at the start of spring. 'The youngster'.

*Fegana*   A mountain stream that flows into the Serchio. 'The asphodel'.

*Fiesole*   The small town in the hills to the north-east of Florence. 'Evening at Fiesole'.

*Fiorenza*   This early form of Firenze (Florence) has suggestions of flowering (Italian *fiorire*) and of Florence's emblem the lily. 'First dithyramb'.

*Fire, everlasting*   The fire which burned always in ancient Rome in honour of Vesta, the goddess of the hearth. 'Dreams of distant places'.

240

*Five regions*   Le Cinque Terre, that is Monterosso, Vernazza, Corniglia, Manarola, and Riomaggiore, on the coast of Liguria near La Spezia. 'August festival'.

*Flautist of the marsh*   A frog. 'The vulture of the Sun'.

*Flautist with the eyes like almonds*   A relief on the Ludovisi Throne in the Baths of Diocletian. 'Dreams of distant places'.

*Florentine*   In 'that Aretusa who was Florentine' d'Annunzio is stressing that this is a mortal woman. See Arethuse / Aretusa. 'The oleander'.

*Florentine Muse*   The poetic genius of Florence, its poetry, and its poets. 'The youngster'.

*Florence, city in flower*   This alludes to Florence's emblem the lily and also to a derivation of the name of the city from *fiorire*, to flower. 'First dithyramb'.

*Flowering city*   This alludes to Florence's emblem the lily and also to a derivation of the name of the city from *fiorire*, to flower. 'The youngster'.

*Flute, double*   An instrument made of two tubes, held one in each of the musician's hands, which come together at the mouthpiece. 'The youngster', 'Dreams of distant places'.

*Flutes, wingèd*   Crickets. 'The tributaries'.

*Fluvial*   Of a river. The 'fluvial ode' mentioned in 'The coronal of Glauco' is the poem 'Between two Arnos'. 'Mouth of the Serchio', 'The stag', 'The coronal of Glauco', 'The goatskin'.

*Fluviale*   Probably best understood as d'Annunzio's name for the god of the River Arno. It may, however, refer to his companion in this poem: in an earlier version the name used was Ermione. 'The tributaries'.

*Folo*   Glauco's horse. 'Mouth of the Serchio', 'The hippocampus'.

*Fondi*   A town in southern Lazio on the shores of a lake. 'First dithyramb'.

*Forci*   A village on the right bank of the Freddana. 'The asphodel'.

*Forum*   The main square of ancient Rome. 'Dreams of distant places'.

241

*Fossa Burlamacca*   A canal which is fed by the marshy waters round Lake Massaciùccoli and which enters the sea near Viareggio. 'Envoi'.

*Fountain of Iuturna*   The spring which rises in the Forum at the foot of the Palatine Hill. Iuturna was an ancient divinity of Lazio. 'Dreams of distant places'.

*Frattetta*   A district to the north of Carrara. 'The asphodel'.

*Freddana*   A mountain stream which flows into the Serchio. 'The asphodel'.

*Frigido*   A river which rises on Mount Tambura. 'The asphodel'.

*Furies*   Divinities of the underworld. 'Terra, vale!'

*Fvrit aestvs*   'The heat [of summer] is raging.' 'Fvrit aestvs'.


*Gàbberi*   A mountain, 'like a metal basinet' because of its shape. 'Envoi'.

*Garbo*   A medium-sized merchant ship used in the Levant. 'Dreams of distant places'.

*Gela's tyrant*   Gelon, praised by Pindar in his first Pythian Ode. 'The prisoner'.

*Germa*   A large merchant ship used in the Levant. 'Dreams of distant places'.

*Giogo di Scarperia*   A mountain near Florence. 'The asphodel'.

*Giovo*   A mountain of the Apuan Alps. 'The highest Alps', 'the asphodel'.

*Glauco*   A mythical Boeotian fisherman who ate a herb which turned him into a sea-god; the word in Italian means glaucous. He represents d'Annunzio's desire for divinity. At times he is identified with the poet, explicitly in 'The coronal of Glauco' with its allusion to 'Between two Arnos', 'that ode of yours / where Procne on her island mourns the rape'. 'Second dithyramb', 'The oleander', 'Mouth of the Serchio', 'The coronal of Glauco', 'The asphodel'.

*Glaucous*   Of a sea-green or greyish blue colour. 'The youngster',
'Dreams of distant places'.

*Goddess with the endless torch*   The Roman goddess of the hearth,
Vesta. Her torch is 'endless' by hyperbole because it is long,
and 'endless' also because the fire which burned in her honour
was never allowed to go out. 'Dreams of distant places'.

*God, lustful garden*   Priapus, the symbol of fertility, usually
represented with a very large ithyphallus. He was propitiated
with gifts of cakes. 'August festival'.

*God, sky-blue*   Glauco. 'Terra, vale!'

*God who guides the chariot of light*   The Sun. 'Fourth dithyramb'.

*Gombo*   The stretch of coast between the mouth of the Arno and
the mouth of the Serchio. 'Noon', 'The mothers', 'The highest
Alps', 'Gombo', 'Orphic anniversary', 'The asphodel'.

*Gorgo*   This name is chosen because it means in Greek 'ardent,
spirited', and also because it sounds like a name from 'The
Greek anthology'. 'The coronal of Glauco'.

*Gorgon*   There were three Gorgons, but the one best known is
Medusa. Pegasus was born from her blood. They were women
with snakes for hair, whose gaze turned people to stone. 'The
oleander', 'Third dithyramb', 'Roman sarcophagus'.

*Gorgona*   With Capraia, an island which Dante implored to move
to block up the mouth of the Arno in order to drown the inhab-
itants of Pisa and so avenge the death of Ugolino. ('Inferno',
XXXIII, 82-84). 'Noon'.

*Grace*   The three Graces were Roman goddesses personifying
beauty and artistic inspiration. 'Peace', 'The name', 'Third
dithyramb'.

*Grateful*   Pleasant, agreeable. 'Works and days', 'Dreams of
distant places'.

*Great Mother*   Cybele, a personification of nature's fecundity.
'First dithyramb'.

*Greve*   A tributary of the Arno. 'The tributaries'.

*Gulf, the*   The Gulf of La Spezia. 'Envoi'.

243

*Hades* The underworld, Avernus, Dis; also the god of the under-world. 'The roots of song', 'The name', 'The asphodel'.

*Halcyon* A species of kingfisher. See Alcỳone. 'A goddess of the shore', 'Undulna'.

*Heald* Part of the equipment used in weaving. 'The goatskin'.

*Hebe* The goddess of youth. Her name was the battle-cry at Mycale. 'The prisoner'.

*Hebrus* The river in Thrace into which the Bacchantes threw the severed head of Orpheus. 'Orphic anniversary', 'The oleander', 'The Victory of Samothrace'.

*Helen* Queen of Sparta, whose abduction was the cause of the Trojan War. 'The name', 'Second dithyramb'.

*Helicon* A Boeotian mountain sacred to Apollo and the Muses. See Muse. 'First dithyramb', 'Summer madrigals'.

*Hellespont(s)* The modern Dardanelles. The 'Sea of Helle' was so called because Helle was drowned there. The use of the word in the plural is an antonomasia for sea straits in general. 'The oleander', 'Fourth dithyramb'.

*Herd, lazy* The constellation Boötes. The herdsman is 'lazy' because the constellation is slow to set. 'Envoi'.

*Hermes* The messenger of the gods, represented with a winged hat and winged boots. He had the duty of conducting the shades of the dead to Hades. 'Fourth dithyramb', 'Dreams of distant places'.

*Hero born from gold* Perseus, the son of Danae and of Zeus who came to her in a shower of gold. 'The many-headed song'.

*Hesperis* One of the Hesperides, the guardians of a tree which provided golden apples. 'Third dithyramb'.

*Hesperus* The evening star. 'August festival'.

*Hieron* King of Syracuse, victor in the chariot-race in the Olympic Games in 468 BC. See Bacchylides. 'The oleander'.

*Hippocampus* A sea-horse; also a mythical horse-like sea-monster. 'The hippocampus'.

*Hollows Beyond*   Le Lame di Fuori, the shore on the right bank of the mouth of the Arno. 'The camels', 'The mothers'.

*Horses of the Sun*   The horses drawing the mythical chariot of the sun. 'First dithyramb', 'Fourth dithyramb'.

*Hour(s)*   Roman goddesses who presided at the changing of the seasons. 'Mouth of the Arno', 'The Sea-Hours'.

*Hyacinth*   A Greek youth killed by Apollo and changed into a flower. 'Summer madrigals'.

*Hyas*   Brother of the Pleiades. He was torn to pieces by a lioness whose cubs he had tried to take. 'Before dawn'.

*Hydras*   Freshwater creatures with the power of multiplying when cut up. Also the Hydra was a mythical monster with many heads: when one was cut off two grew in its place. 'The youngster'.

*Hydroscope*   A clepsydra or water-clock. 'The youngster'.

*Hymettus*   A mountain in Attica, famous for its honey. 'The youngster'.

*Hyperion*   The father of Helios (the sun). Sometimes he is himself regarded as the sun. 'Fourth dithyramb'.

*Hypogea*   A hypogeum is a subterranean tomb. 'Noon'.


*Icarus*   He flew with wings made by his father Daedalus. Ignoring his father's warnings, he flew too high, the sun melted the wax which held the feathers together, and he fell into the sea and was drowned. The sea was named after him the Icarian Sea. 'The wing on the sea', 'Altivs egit iter', 'Fourth dithyramb'.

*Ida, Mount*   A mountain in the centre of Crete. 'Fourth dithyramb'.

*Ilissus*   A stream flowing from Mount Hymettus. 'Fourth dithyramb'.

*Ilium*   Troy. 'First dithyramb'.

*Ionia*   An ancient region on the western coast of Asia Minor, settled by Ionian Greeks. It was here that early Greek literature and philosophy were chiefly developed. 'The coronal of Glauco'.

245

*Ionian Sea*   To the west of Greece. 'Envoi'.

*Io Paean*   An invocation of Apollo, used by the Greeks and Romans as a cry of joy. 'First dithyramb', 'The oleander'.

*Iris*   The rainbow goddess. 'Fourth dithyramb'.

*Island of the Lighthouse*   Tino, off the Ligurian coast near Porto-venere. 'Noon'.

*Isthmus, the*   Of Corinth. 'Summer madrigals'.

*Iuturna*   An ancient divinity of Lazio. 'Dreams of distant places'.

*Ixion*   He tried to rape Hera, wife of Zeus; but Zeus substituted a cloud which looked like her. The offspring of this union was the Centaur. 'The death of the stag'.


*Jocasta*   The mother of Antigone. 'Orphic anniversary'.

*Julia*   Her statue is in the museum of the Baths of Diocletian. 'Dreams of distant places'.


*King of deceits*   This is the husband of Procne, Tereus, who raped her sister Philomela. Procne became a swallow and Philomela a nightingale. 'Between two Arnos'.

*Knossos*   One of the most important cities of ancient Crete. 'Fourth dithyramb'.


*Labyrinth, great*   Constructed by Daedalus in Crete. 'Fourth dithyramb'.

*Lacus Iuturnae*   This is Iuturnae fons or the Fountain of Iuturna. 'Dreams of distant places'.

*Lacustrial*   Lacustral, lacustrine, of a lake or lakes. 'First dithyramb'.

*Lady, solar*   A description used for Pasiphae and for Circe, who were both daughters of the Sun. 'Mouth of the Serchio', 'Fourth dithyramb'.

*Laocoön*   The name of the priest who was killed by sea-serpents as he tried to dissuade the Trojans from allowing the wooden horse into Troy. 'The truce'.

246

*La Spezia*   A naval base on the Ligurian coast. 'Envoi'.

*Latinus*   King of Latium (modern Lazio) who became the father-in-law of Aeneas. In a courtyard of his palace there was a laurel he had dedicated to Apollo at the time when the palace was being built. 'First dithyramb'.

*La Verna*   A mountain group in the Apennines. It is famous as the place where Saint Francis received the stigmata. 'The tributaries', 'The asphodel'.

*Lavinia*   The daugher of Latinus. 'First dithyramb'.

*Lazio*   The region of Italy which includes Rome. 'First dithyramb', 'Dreams of distant places'.

*Leda*   The mother of Helen. 'The name'.

*Leonardo*   Leonardo da Vinci. 'Dreams of distant places'.

*Leontini*   Now Lentini, in Sicily. 'The two eyes of a Pleiad'.

*Leo, sun in*   24 July-23 August. 'The tenzon'.

*Lethe*   The river in Hades from which the dead drank to make them forget their earthly life. 'Fourth dithyramb'.

*Lethean lady*   Proserpina. 'The asphodel'.

*Liber*   Bacchus, the god of wine. 'First dithyramb', 'The goatskin'.

*Lighthouse Island*   Tino, off the Ligurian coast near Portovenere. 'August festival'.

*Lily of power*   The lily is the emblem of Florence. 'First dithyramb'.

*Liminary*   At the edge or threshold. 'Mouth of the Serchio'.

*Liri*   The river which is the boundary between Lazio and the region to the south of it, Campania. 'First dithyramb'.

*Livorno*   Leghorn, on the coast of Tuscany south of Pisa. 'Noon'.

*Lombard(ic) plain*   In the far north of Italy. 'Dreams of distant places'.

*Lord*   Like Daemon, Despot, Emperor, and Master, the poet's own genius, the inner voice whose commands must be obeyed. 'Altivs egit iter'.

*Lorenzo*   Lorenzo de' Medici (1449-1492). 'The youngster', 'The tributaries'.

*Loricino*   A small river in Lazio. 'Dreams of distant places'.

*Lower Sea*   The ancient Roman name for the Tyrrhene Sea. 'First dithyramb', 'Second dithyramb', 'Envoi'.

*Luca della Robbia*   Florentine sculptor (1400-1482). 'The youngster'.

*Luna*   The Roman goddess of the moon. 'By the side of the Affrico on an evening in June after rain', 'New moon'.

*Luni*   An ancient Etruscan town on the left bank of the Magra, near modern Sarzana, with the Apuan Alps nearby. 'The mothers', 'Calm', 'The highest Alps', 'Orphic anniversary', 'The oleander', 'The coronal of Glauco', 'Triton', 'Roman sarcophagus', 'The rupestrian peplos', 'Envoi'.

*Lunigiana*   The district round the Magra. 'The asphodel'.

*Lustral*   Purifying. 'The olive', 'Second dithyramb'.

*Lybian south winds*   The sirocco. 'First dithyramb'.

*Lycia*   A region of Asia Minor. 'The two eyes of a Pleiad'.

*Lydian sand*   The sand mingled with gold dust of the River Pactolus in Lydia in Asia Minor. 'The coronal of Glauco'.

*Lyrist, imperial*   Nero, who enjoyed playing the lyre, had a palace at Anzio. 'Dreams of distant places'.


*Maculate*   Spotted, dappled. 'First dithyramb'.

*Maenads*   Bacchantes. 'Dreams of distant places'.

*Magno, Monte*   A hill to the south-east of Camaiore. 'Envoi'.

*Magra*   A river which forms the northern boundary of Versilia. 'Orphic anniversary', 'August festival', 'Undulna'.

*Maiden*   The sun is in the sign of Virgo (the Maiden) 24 August-23 September. 'Undulna'.

*Manes*   The shade of a dead person. (The word is Latin and pronounced with two syllables.) 'The asphodel'.

*Maremma / Maremme*   In the singular or the plural, this is the coastal area partly in Tuscany and partly in Lazio which was formerly marshy but is now reclaimed. 'The ear of corn', 'First dithyramb', 'The asphodel'.

*Mare Nostrum*   'Our sea', the ancient Roman name for the Mediterranean. 'Orphic anniversary'.

*Marica*   A nymph, the mother of Latinus. 'First dithyramb'.

*Marina di Pisa*   The shore between the mouth of the Arno and the mouth of the Serchio. 'The tenzon'.

*Marinella di Luni*   A village near the mouth of the Magra, near the remains of Luni. 'The asphodel'.

*Mario's shade*   Mario or Marius (157-86 BC), a Roman soldier and consul, during his conflict with Sulla hid in the marshes of Minturno. 'First dithyramb'.

*Marpessos*   A Greek mountain famous for its white marble. 'Fourth dithyramb'.

*Marsyas*   A satyr who, proud of his flute-playing, challenged Apollo to a musical contest. Apollo won, and then he tied Marsyas to a pine and flayed him alive. 'The coronal of Glauco', 'The goatskin'.

*Massaciùccoli, Lake*   In Tuscany near Viareggio. 'The coronal of Glauco', 'Envoi'.

*Massic*   A wine, famous among the ancient Romans, made from vines grown on Mount Massico in Campania. 'First dithyramb'.

*Master*   Like Daemon, Despot, Emperor, and Lord, the poet's own genius, the inner voice whose commands must be obeyed. 'The truce'.

*Matanna*   A mountain in the Apuan Alps. 'Envoi'.

*Maze, the*   Constructed by Daedalus in Crete. 'Fourth dithyramb'.

*Mede*   The Medes (Persians) were notorious among the ancient Romans for their effeminacy. 'Envoi'.

*Medusa(e)*   The best known Gorgon. It is also a jellyfish, so called from the resemblance of its filaments to the snaky hair of

249

Medusa. 'The hippocampus', 'Third dithyramb', 'The many-headed song', 'Roman sarcophagus', 'Undulna', 'New moon'.

*Mèlitta*   This name is chosen because it means in Greek 'honey' and because it sounds like a name from the 'Greek anthology'. 'The coronal of Glauco'.

*Mensola*   A tributary of the Arno. 'The youngster'.

*Midas*   Celebrated by Pindar. 'The many-headed song'.

*Minos*   King of Crete, husband of Pasiphae. 'The wing on the sea'.

*Minturno*   Town in Lazio. 'First dithyramb'.

*Mommio, (Mount)*   A hill south of Camaiore. 'The asphodel', 'Envoi'.

*Montràmito*   A hill near Camaiore. 'The coronal of Glauco'.

*Motrone*   A stream which enters the Tyrrhene Sea near Marina di Pietrasanta. 'Summer madrigals'.

*Mugello*   The valley of the River Sieve to the north of Florence. 'The asphodel'.

*Mull*   Used as the name of a fish. 'The coronal of Glauco'.

*Muse*   The Muses, usually said to be nine in number, were Greek goddesses of literature and the arts. 'The hippocampus', 'Third dithyramb'.

*Musicians, ephemeral*   Puffs of wind. 'Mouth of the Serchio'.

*Must*   New wine. 'First dithyramb', 'New moon'.

*Mycale*   A promontory in Asia Minor where the Greeks destroyed a Persian army and fleet in 479 BC. 'The prisoner'.


*Nephele*   This Greek name means 'cloud'. 'Fourth dithyramb'.

*Neptune's tomb*   The temple at Onchestus dedicated to Neptune, the Roman god of the sea, is referred to as a 'tomb' because the cult of Neptune is now dead. 'Summer madrigals'.

*Nereids*   Sea-nymphs. 'Peace'.

*Neumes*  In medieval music, signs giving an indication of rise or fall of pitch. 'Undulna'.

*Nicarete*  A name taken from the 'Greek anthology'. 'The coronal of Glauco'.

*Nico*  A name taken from the 'Greek anthology'. 'The coronal of Glauco'.

*Nightingale of Ceos*  Bacchylides. 'The oleander'.

*Nike*  The Greek personification of Victory, represented as winged and flying very fast. The famous statue of Nike found at Samothrace has lost its head and arms. 'The oleander', 'The rupestrian peplos', 'Fourth dithyramb'.

*Niobe*  Niobe, proud of her fourteen children, mocked Latona who had only two children, Apollo and Diana. As a punishment Latona's children killed all Niobe's in one day. Niobe wept herself to death and was turned into stone. 'Gombo', 'Orphic anniversary'.

*Nymphine*  Inhabited by a nymph. 'The oleander'.


*Obolus*  An ancient Greek coin. 'The name'.

*Oceanid(s)*  Sea-nymph(s). 'The asphodel', 'Fourth dithyramb'.

*Ocean laurel*  Sargasso or gulfweed. 'Ocean laurel'.

*Ocean, old*  Oceanus, the personification of the sea which the early Greeks believed surrounded the world. 'Before dawn'.

*Odysseus*  A proverbial restless wanderer, the mythical king of the small Greek island of Ithaca. Two of his adventures particularly are mentioned by d'Annunzio: with Circe, who turned his companions into swine, but was successfully resisted by Odysseus himself; with the Sirens, when Odysseus was able to sail past them and hear their seductive singing unharmed because he had filled his companions' ears with wax and had had himself bound to the mast of his ship. 'First dithyramb', 'The oleander'.

*Oleggio*  A town on the Ticino. 'Dreams of distant places'.

*Olympus*   A mountain overlooking the Vale of Tempe in Greece through which the Peneios flows. 'The oleander'.

*Ombrone*   A tributary of the Arno. See Ambra. 'The youngster', 'The tributaries'.

*Onchestus*   A Boeotian city. 'Summer madrigals'.

*Orchomenus*   A Boeotian city. 'The many-headed song'.

*Orion*   A mythical Greek hunter who on his death became a constellation in which he is seen as a giant with belt and sword. 'Before dawn', 'The oleander', 'Envoi'.

*Orpheus*   A mythical Thracian poet who could charm animals and even inanimate things by the music of his lyre. He sailed with other heroes on the Argo. His grief at the death of his wife Eurydice so enraged some Bacchantes that they tore him to pieces. His head was thrown into the River Hebrus and carried out to sea. The 'sky-blue Orpheus' of 'The asphodel' is an antonomasia for Shelley who had blue eyes. 'Orphic anniversary', 'Second dithyramb', 'The oleander', 'The asphodel', 'The goatskin', 'Dreams of distant places'.

*Ortygia*   See Arethuse/ Aretusa. 'The oleander'.

*Ossa*   A mountain near Olympus. 'The oleander'.

*Ostia*   Not the modern seaside resort, but the ancient port for Rome nearby, Ostia Antica, now in ruins. 'First dithyramb', 'Mouth of the Serchio'.


*Palatine*   The hill on which Rome was founded. Its 'pale reddish dome' is the brick ruins on top of it. 'Dreams of distant places'.

*Palladian*   Of Pallas (Athene). The 'Palladian silver' of 'Stabat nvda Aestas' is the foliage of the olive. 'Stabat nvda Aestas', 'The goatskin', 'Envoi'.

*Pallas (Athene)*   The chaste Greek goddess, patroness of many arts and protectress of many towns, to whom the olive was sacred. 'The olive', 'The ear of corn', 'The oleander', 'The many-headed song', 'The goatskin'.

*Palmaria*   The largest of the islands at the entrance to the Gulf of La Spezia. 'Envoi'.

*Pan*   The Greek god of flocks and shepherds, a symbol of nature, he is sometimes seen as the embodiment of the universe; his name means 'the whole'. He is represented as a man with horns on his head and with the legs of a goat. He is often shown playing a double flute or a syrinx. Especially at midday he could be alarming with the sound of his music and his loud voice. Sometimes he is identified with Faunus. 'Works and days', 'First dithyramb', 'The coronal of Glauco', 'Third dithyramb', 'August festival', 'Fourth dithyramb'.

*Panathenaea*   A festival and games in honour of Pallas (Athene). 'The youngster'.

*Pancrazio*   The pancratium or pancration was an ancient Greek athletic contest combining wrestling and boxing. Pancratium maritimum is the name of a kind of white lily. 'Orphic anniversary', 'The asphodel', 'Undulna', 'Envoi'.

*Pania*   A mountain of the Apuan Alps. 'The highest Alps', 'August festival', 'Undulna', 'Envoi'.

*Paphlagonian*   Paphlagonia was a region on the southern shore of the Black Sea, a source of slaves for ancient Greece. Paphlagon is a character in Aristophanes' 'Knights', a dealer in leather who whips other slaves. 'The coronal of Glauco'.

*Parenzo*   A town in Istria. See Capodistria. 'Dreams of distant places'.

*Parian*   Of Paros. 'Dreams of distant places'.

*Parnes, Mount*   In the northern part of Attica. 'The youngster'.

*Paros*   An island in the Cyclades famed for its white marble. 'Fourth dithyramb'.

*Pasiphae*   The wife of Minos of Crete, she lusted for a white bull. See Daedalus. 'Fourth dithyramb'.

*P.B.S.*   Percy Bysshe Shelley. On 8 July 1822 he was drowned while sailing near La Spezia. 'Orphic anniversary'.

*Pegasus*   A mythical winged horse born from the blood of the Gorgon Medusa. It is often used as a symbol of the imagination. 'First dithyramb', 'The oleander', 'Mouth of the Serchio'.

*Pelops*   A mythical king of Elis in Greece who had one shoulder made of ivory. 'The goatskin'.

*Peneios*   A river which flows through the Vale of Tempe in Greece; also the god of this river. See Daphne. 'The oleander'.

*Pentelicus*   A mountain chain to the north-east of Athens, quarried for marble. 'The youngster'.

*Peplos*   In ancient Greece, a long loose garment for women. 'The rupestrian peplos', 'Envoi'.

*Pericles' great father*   Xanthippus, the commander of the Athenian fleet at Mycale. 'The prisoner'.

*Perseis*   The daughter of Ocean and mother of Pasiphae. 'Fourth dithyramb'.

*Pesa*   A tributary of the Arno. 'The tributaries'.

*Pescia*   A tributary of the Arno. 'The tributaries'.

*Phaedimus*   A son of Niobe. 'Gombo'.

*Phalerum*   A port of Athens. 'The youngster'.

*Phlegon*   One of the horses which pulled the chariot of the sun. 'Fourth dithyramb'.

*Phoebus (Apollo)*   See Apollo (Phoebus).

*Phrygian*   Phrygia was a region in the north-west of Asia Minor. The Phrygian mode in music was stirring and emotional. 'The coronal of Glauco', 'Undulna'.

*Phtia*   A daughter of Niobe. 'Gombo'.

*Pietrapana*   Mount Pania. 'Versilia'.

*Pietrasanta*   A town to the north of Viareggio. 'Envoi'.

*Pieve di Camaiore*   In the southern part of the Apuan Alps. 'The asphodel'.

*Pindar*   A Greek lyric poet (518-438 BC) famous for his odes in praise of victorious athletes. 'The oleander'.

*Pirano*   A town in Istria. See Capodistria. 'Dreams of distant places'.

*Pirois*  One of the horses which pulled the chariot of the sun. 'Fourth dithyramb'.

*Pisa*  On the Arno, near its mouth. 'The camels'.

*Pisan Hills*  The squat rounded hills near Pisa. 'Noon', 'The highest Alps', 'Mouth of the Serchio'.

*Plato*  This ancient Greek philosopher became known in Florence, along with other Greek authors, at the time of the Renaissance. 'The youngster'.

*Pleiad(es)*  The Pleiades are a constellation: seven sisters who were changed into stars after the death of their brother Hyas. One Pleiad is not visible, hiding for shame, it was said, because she had been loved by a mortal. Since the morning rising of this constellation marks the beginning of summer, and its morning setting the beginning of autumn, it was regarded as presiding over navigation and agriculture. 'Before dawn', 'The two eyes of a Pleiad', 'The oleander', 'Envoi'.

*Pollux*  See Twins, (Heavenly). 'Second dithyramb'.

*Pontiff who made war*  Pope Julius II, a patron of Michelangelo. 'The prisoner'.

*Populonia*  An ancient Etruscan town on the coast of Tuscany near to Piombino. 'Orphic anniversary', 'The coronal of Glauco', 'The asphodel'.

*Porta Capena*  One of the main gates of ancient Rome. 'First dithyramb'.

*Poseidon*  The Greek god of the sea. Angry that a white bull had not been offered to him in sacrifice, he caused Pasiphae to become enamoured of it. 'Fourth dithyramb'.

*Pratomagno*  A mountain chain of the Apennines in Tuscany. 'The tributaries'.

*Praetor*  A magistrate in ancient Rome. The one alluded to here is C. Lucretius, mentioned by Livy, who had a villa by the Loricino. 'Dreams of distant places'.

*Preneste*  The modern Palestrina, a town east of Rome, a cool place in summer. 'First dithyramb'.

255

*Prisoner*   One of the two naked Prisoners sculptured by Michelangelo for the tomb of Pope Julius II. 'The prisoner'.

*Procne*   'Procne's isle' is 'the island of swallows'. See King of deceits. 'Between two Arnos', 'The coronal of Glauco'.

*Promethean materials / matter*   Marble from the Apuan Alps from which a sculptor can make statues as Prometheus made from clay the first men. 'The highest Alps', 'Envoi'.

*Prometheus*   He made the first men out of clay. For stealing fire from heaven he was punished by being chained to a rock in the Caucasus while a vulture ate his liver which was continually renewed. 'Orphic anniversary'.

*Propylaea*   The entrance to the Acropolis of Athens. 'The youngster'.

*Proserpina / Proserpine*   See Core. 'First dithyramb', 'Third Dithyramb'.

*Pythian, the*   The first of Pindar's Pythian Odes (composed in honour of victors in the Pythian Games). 'The prisoner'.


*Quarrel(s)*   A quarrel is an arrow or cross-bow bolt. In 'The tributaries' and 'Undulna' it is a metaphor for the rays of the sun. 'The truce', 'The tributaries', 'Orphic anniversary', 'Undulna'.

*Quiesa*   A hill by Lake Massaciùccoli near Viareggio. 'The coronal of Glauco', 'Envoi'.


*Rialto*   A district of Venice. 'Dreams of distant places'.

*River, fabled*   The Arno. 'Evening at Fiesole'.

*Romae frvgiferae dic*   'Dedicated to Rome and its fruitfulness'. 'First dithyramb'.

*Romulus*   The legendary founder of Rome. 'First dithyramb'.

*Rucellai Gardens*   In Florence. 'The youngster'.

*Rupestrian*   Made of rock. 'The rupestrian peplos'.

*Sacred Way*   The ancient street which runs through the Forum in Rome. 'Dreams of distant places'.

*Saffron*   In 'August festival' this simply denotes the colour saffron. Elsewhere it is a flower, the autumn crocus, whose blooming is a sign that summer is over. 'The asphodel', 'Summer madrigals', 'August festival', 'The goatskin', 'The signs'.

*Sagittarius*   Archer. 'Fourth dithyramb'.

*Sagro, (Mount)*   In the Apuan Alps, quarried for marble. 'The highest Alps', 'The asphodel', 'The prisoner', 'Envoi'.

*Saica*   A merchant ship used in the Levant. 'Dreams of distant places'.

*Salamis*   The island which gave its name to the sea battle in 480 BC in which the Greeks defeated the Persians. 'The youngster'.

*Samothrace*   An island in the Aegean Sea. The Victory of Samothrace is a famous statue of Nike found there, imagined here as a figurehead. 'The Victory of Samothrace'.

*San Marco, ruins of*   The buildings which preserve the memory of Venetian rule in Capodistria. The winged lion of Saint Mark is the emblem of Venice. 'Dreams of distant places'.

*San Rossore*   A very large estate near Pisa. 'The tenzon', 'Noon', 'The mothers'.

*Sappho*   The Greek poetess from Lesbos who lived around 600 BC. Her 'new song' is one sung in the poem 'Solon', one in which Giovanni Pascoli (1855-1912) worked from fragments of Sappho but produced a poem of his own. 'Envoi'.

*Sargasso Sea*   A floating expanse of gulfweed in the North Atlantic. 'Ocean laurel'.

*Satraps*   Governors of ancient Persian provinces. 'The goatskin'.

*Saturnian City*   Rome. Saturn was a very old Italian god who was said to have founded a village on the site of the future city of Rome. 'First dithyramb'.

*Satyr*   A woodland deity, half man and half goat. 'Versilia', 'The goatskin'.

*Scales*   The sun is in the constellation Libra (the Scales or Balance) 24 September-23 October, when day and night are equal. 'The asphodel', 'Undulna'.

*Schirazzo*   A light merchant ship with square sails, used at one time by the Turks and Venetians. 'Dreams of distant places'.

*Scorpio*   The sun is in the constellation Scorpio (the Scorpion) 24 October-22 November. 'The asphodel'.

*Scythian*   The Scythians lived to the north of the Black Sea. The ancient Romans considered them coarse and stupid. 'Envoi'.

*Selene*   The Greek goddess of the moon. 'New moon'.

*Sequence*   A hymn in rhythmical prose. 'Dreams of distant places'.

*Serchio*   The river which marks the southern limit of Versilia. 'Noon', 'The mothers', 'Orphic anniversary', 'Mouth of the Serchio', 'The stag', 'The coronal of Glauco', 'Versilia', 'The death of the stag', 'The asphodel', 'August festival', 'Undulna', 'The goatskin', 'Envoi'.

*'Serene', stone said to be*   *Pietra serena*, a grey-blue stone. 'Works and days'.

*Sesto Calende*   A town in Lombardy. 'Dreams of distant places'.

*Shepherd King*   An Egyptian statue of a king of the Hyksos dynasty. 'Dreams of distant places'.

*Sibyl*   A priestess who spoke the oracles of Apollo. See Aeneas. 'Envoi'.

*Sieve*   A tributary of the Arno. 'The tributaries'.

*Siliqua*   A pod. 'Dreams of distant places'.

*Silver Bow*   An Homeric term for Apollo. 'The oleander'.

*Simonetta*   Simonetta Cattaneo, loved by Giuliano de' Medici and celebrated by Poliziano and Botticelli, who died young. 'First dithyramb', 'Peace'.

*Sinopia*   A kind of reddish ochre. 'First dithyramb'.

*Sinuessa*   An ancient town in Lazio near to its border with Campania. 'First dithyramb'.

*Siren(s), Syren* The sirens were sea demons, half woman and half bird, who attracted sailors into danger with their singing. 'The youngster', 'The oleander', 'The hippocampus', 'Summer madrigals', 'The Sea-Hours'.

*Sirius* The dogstar. The period when it rises with the sun (July and the early part of August) is proverbially very hot. 'Fourth dithyramb'.

*Skep* A beehive. 'Peace'.

*Sophocles* According to legend the Greek dramatist Sophocles (496-406 BC) was fed with honey by bees when he was in his cradle. Shelley had a volume of Sophocles in his pocket when he was drowned. 'Orphic anniversary'.

*Sophocles' nightingales* See Antigone. 'The youngster'.

*Soraggio's Mount* In the upper valley of the Serchio. 'The asphodel'.

*Stabat nvda Aestas* 'Summer was naked'. 'Stabat nvda Aestas'.

*Stater* An ancient Greek coin. 'The two eyes of a Pleiad'.

*Stheno* A Gorgon, sister of Medusa. 'The many-headed song'.

*Strymonian* From the River Strymon in Macedonia. 'Fourth dithyramb'.

*Stygian* Of the Styx. 'The goatskin'.

*Styx* A river of Hades, across which the shades of the dead were ferried. 'The name'.

*Succinct* Girded up. 'The youngster'.

*Syracuse* One of the first Greek cities to be founded in Sicily. The 'golden effigy' is on a coin. 'The oleander'.

*Syrinx(es)* Syrinx was a nymph who, when pursued by Pan, prayed successfully to be changed into a reed. A syrinx is also Pan-pipes. 'Summer madrigals', 'August festival'.

*Syrtes* Quicksands. 'The oleander'.

*Tambura* A mountain in the Apuan Alps. 'The highest Alps', 'The asphodel'.

*Tanagra*   A town in Boeotia. 'August festival'.

*Tangle*   A kind of seaweed. 'Noon', 'Terra, vale!', 'The coronal of Glauco', 'Undulna'.

*Tarpeia*   The Vestal who, according to legend, betrayed the Capitol at Rome to the Sabines. She gave her name to the Tarpeian Rock on the Capitoline Hill, from which criminals were thrown. 'Dreams of distant places'.

*Tartarus*   The underworld, especially when thought of as a place of punishment. 'Second dithyramb'.

*Tead*   In antiquity a torch made from a branch of a resinous bush or tree, used especially on ceremonial occasions. 'August festival', 'The vulture of the Sun'.

*Tenzon*   A singing contest. 'Peace', 'The tenzon'.

*Tereglio*   A village in the valley of the Serchio. 'The asphodel'.

*Terra, vale!*   'Earth, goodbye!' 'Terra, vale!', 'Second dithyramb'.

*Tetradrachm*   An ancient Greek coin. 'The two eyes of a Pleiad'.

*Thebes*   The main city in Boeotia. 'The oleander', 'The prisoner'.

*Thera*   A daughter of Niobe. 'Gombo'.

*Thespia*   A city in Boeotia, destroyed by Thebes. 'The prisoner'.

*Thessalian*   Of Thessaly. 'The two eyes of a Pleiad', 'The death of the stag', 'The Thessalian'.

*Thessaly*   A region of Greece, famous for its horse-breeding, and where the Centaur was said to live. 'The oleander', 'The coronal of Glauco', 'The Thessalian'.

*Thetis*   A Greek sea-goddess. 'Undulna'.

*Thousand-headed melody*   According to Pindar (in the twelfth of his Pythian Odes) this was invented by Pallas in imitation of the many sounds which, when the Gorgon Medusa was killed, came from the snake-haired heads of her sisters. 'The many-headed song'.

*Thrace, swallow from*   Procne. Thrace was to the north of Greece. 'Between two Arnos'.

*Thracian*   Orpheus was from Thrace. 'Orphic anniversary', 'Second dithyramb', 'The goatskin'.

*Thunderer*   Zeus, the king of the ancient Greek gods. 'The highest Alps'.

*Thyrsus, Thyrsi*   The thyrsus was a staff, tipped with a pine cone and wreathed with vine and ivy leaves, carried by Dionysus and his votaries the Bacchantes. 'The coronal of Glauco', 'The death of the stag', 'Fourth dithyramb'.

*Ticino*   A river which flows south out of Lago Maggiore, passing to the west of Milan. 'Dreams of distant places'.

*Titan*   The sun. 'First dithyramb', 'Third dithyramb'.

*Tityrus*   A character in Virgil's 'Eclogues'. 'Envoi'.

*Toscana*   The region of Italy in which most of these poems are set. It lies to the north of Lazio, and its chief town is Florence. The name is anglicized as Tuscany. 'Peace'.

*Towers, two*   The tower of 'prayer' is the bell-tower of the cathedral in Florence, and the tower 'of authority' is the tower of the Palazzo della Signoria. 'Beatitude'.

*Travertine*   A pale limestone. 'Dreams of distant places'.

*Trieste*   The largest port on the Adriatic. It was Austrian when d'Annunzio was writing before the First World War, it was ceded to Italy after that war, it became independent in 1945, and it was returned to Italy in 1954. 'Dreams of distant places'.

*Triton*   A sea-god represented as a man with the tail of a fish. 'Orphic anniversary', 'The coronal of Glauco', 'Triton', 'The Sea-Hours'.

*Tritonian*   Of Triton. 'Second dithyramb'.

*Tuffa*   Rock composed of volcanic fragments. 'Dreams of distant places'.

*Turnus*   In the 'Aeneid', the King of the Rutuli who unsuccessfully resisted Aeneas's settlement in Italy. 'First dithyramb'.

*Tuscany*   See Toscana. 'First dithyramb', 'Versilia'.

*Tuscolo*   The remains of this city lie a few miles south-east of Rome. 'First dithyramb'.

*Tyrrhene / Tyrrhenian (Sea)*   To the west of Italy. D'Annunzio also calls it the Etruscan Sea and the Lower Sea. 'First dithyramb', 'Peace', 'The highest Alps', 'Orphic anniversary', 'The oleander', 'Mouth of the Serchio', 'The coronal of Glauco', 'Third dithyramb', 'Summer madrigals', 'Envoi'.

*Twins, (Heavenly)*   Castor and Pollux, gods who according to legend helped the Romans win the Battle of Lake Regillus against the Latins in about 496 BC. 'Dreams of distant places'.

*Uberous*   Giving abundance of milk. 'The goatskin'.

*Uccellina*   A hill in Maremma near Grosseto. 'The asphodel'.

*Uffente*   A watercourse which runs into the Pontine Marches. 'Dreams of distant places'.

*Umbrina*   A fish. 'August festival'.

*Undulna*   Like Versilia, a character invented by d'Annunzio who reveals her own nature as she speaks. The name is probably derived from the Latin word for a wave. 'A goddess of the shore', 'Undulna'.

*Uranian*   Heavenly. 'August festival'.

*Val di Magra*   Lunigiana, the valley of the River Magra which marks the northern limit of Versilia. 'August festival', 'Envoi'.

*Val di Serchio*   The valley of the River Serchio which marks the southern limit of Versilia. 'Envoi'.

*Vara*   A tributary of the River Magra. 'Envoi'.

*Vecchiano*   A district between the Serchio and the Pisan Hills. 'Mouth of the Serchio'.

*Vella*   A stream which flows into the River Gizio near Sulmona in Abruzzi. 'Dreams of distant places'.

*Venus*   The Roman goddess of love. 'The rain in the pine wood', 'The name'.

*Venus, son of*   Aeneas. 'First dithyramb'.

*Vernazza*  A town of the Five Regions, famous for its wine. 'August festival'.

*Versilia*  Like Undulna, a character invented by d'Annunzio who reveals her own nature as she speaks. He did not invent the name: Versilia is the Tuscan coastal region between the River Magra and the River Serchio, and it is also a river which runs through this region. 'Versilia', 'Envoi'.

*Vertumnus*  A Roman god who was said to be able to take any shape he wished. 'The goatskin'.

*Vesta*  The Roman goddess of the hearth and of family life. 'The ear of corn'.

*Vestal*  A Vestal Virgin, one of the 'guardians of the everlasting Fire' in the temple of Vesta. 'Dreams of distant places'.

*Victory*  Nike, the Greek personification of Victory, represented as winged and flying very fast. Three effigies of her are referred to in 'The youngster': 'wingless Victory' whose wings had been clipped by the Athenians so that she could not abandon their city; a Victory 'by whom the bull is pulled' to sacrifice; and a Victory pictured in the act of undoing her sandals. 'The youngster', 'The olive', 'The Victory of Samothrace'.

*Virgil's last and greatest child*  The poet Giovanni Pascoli (1855-1912). 'Envoi'.

*Virid*  Green. 'The wave'.

*Volsci*  The people who once lived in the north-east of Lazio. 'First dithyramb'.

*Volturno*  A river in Campania. 'First dithyramb'.

*Vulcanic*  Volcanic, red-hot. 'First dithyramb'.

*Vulnerary*  Useful in healing wounds. 'Fourth dithyramb'.


*Walls the Arno parts*  The walls of Florence. 'The youngster'.

*Witch, greedy*  Circe. 'First dithyramb'.